THE GOLDEN WINGS
An Anthology of World Poetry

THE GOLDEN WINGS
An Anthology of World Poetry

Edited by
Santosh Kumar

CYBERWIT. NET
2002

THE GOLDEN WINGS
An Anthology of World Poetry

Editor-In-Chief
Dr. Santosh Kumar

Assistant Editor
Dr. Nilanshu Kumar Agrawal

Managing Editor
Radha Agrawal

Deputy Managing Editor
Karunesh Kumar Agrawal

Editorial Advisor
Shikha

Published By
Cyberwit.net
4/2B, L.I.G. Govindpur Colony,
Allahabad-211004
(U.P.) India
Tel: 91-532-541153
E-mail: cyberwit@rediffmail.com

ISBN 81-901366-1-5

World copyright of each poem rests with author.
The views of contributing poets are not necessarily the views of the publisher and the editors.

Note: The Golden Wings is a work of fiction and non-fiction. Characters, places, and incidents are created by the poet's imagination, and any resemblance to actual persons, living or dead, events, or locales is entirely coincidental.

Typeset by Image, 90/ 1, B. K. Banerji Marg, New Katra, Allahabad
Printed in India at Graphic Offset, Tagore Town, Allahabad

The poet's eye, in a fine frenzy rolling,
Doth glance from heaven to earth, from earth to heaven;
And, as imagination bodies forth
The form of things unknown, the poet's pen
Turns them to shapes, and gives to airy nothings
A local habitation and a name.

—Shakespeare

PREFACE

Poetry, like other arts, produces a unique joy through an artistic creation of beauty. To such artistic creation each poet included in *The Golden Wings* brings a freshness and individuality that give the poems an original place in world poetry. Poets differ in their moods; spring is "the cruelest month" for T.S. Eliot. On the contrary April is energetic and cheerful for Chaucer in Prologue to *The Canterbury Tales*. But it may be remembered that a poet should write without interruption from the intrusion of his personal peculiarities. Arnold calls the artist "most fortunate, when he most entirely succeeds in effacing himself." "The progress of an artist is a continual extinction of personality." (T.S. Eliot)

Some of the poets included in *The Golden Wings* may well become the idols of intellectuals; some might become immortal like Eliot, Pound, William Carlos Williams, Marianne Moore, Wallace Stevens. Who can forget the poems of Kenneth Patchen, Muriel Rukeyser, Elizabeth Bishop, Babette Deutsch, Richard Eberhart, Theodore Roethke, Randall Jarrell, Delmore Schwartz, Robert Lowell, Richard Wilbur? The mysticism of these American poets' inspiration and symbolism of their vision is extraordinary. The poets like Bob Dylan, Donovan, Simon and Garfunkel, Richard Farina and others have put English poetry on a new strength and beauty.

Some poets in *The Golden Wings* appear to discover beauty in the most concrete terms possible. Experience itself seems to be their aim. They write about some irresistibly real and attractive mood or passion, some most enchanting object of nature. This is possible only when the poet is free from all prejudices, and open to all impressions of all kinds. Pater aptly pointed out that the true function of art is "to give nothing but the highest quality to your moments as they pass, and simply for those moments' sake." In fact, writing a poem is a happy moment in itself, an ecstatic and best moment, a kind of spiritual discovery for the poet while concentrating on inner experience. The subtle sense of the unknown and a rapture created by manifestations of beauty wherever they may be found help a poet to get away from the pressure of brutal reality. No doubt, Imagism was a reaction against such romanticism. T. E. Hulme wisely asserted the importance of "hard, dry image" in poetry. The

Imagists like Ezra Pound, Hilda Doolittle, Amy Lowell, F.S. Flint aimed at creating "hard, brilliant, clear effects instead of the soft, dreamy vagueness of the hollow Miltonic rhetoric." The Imagists overemphasized the technique and neglected the content. Next, the surrealistic poets were concerned with madness, hypnosis and hallucination; a higher reality could be apprehended only by freeing the mind from logic and rational control.

Now the question arises whether the world poets should express themselves through violent distortions and exaggerations to the point of excess. It is evident that poetry is not "a turning loose of emotions." One must remember that Shakespeare transmuted personal agonies into universal emotions. In fact, each great poet strives to escape from the burden of private life. Instead of indulging in romantic self exploitation, the poets in *The Golden Wings* have written in altered rhythm. No doubt, the traumatic experience of naked terrorism and the dark clouds of a nuclear war have greatly affected the poet. Terrorism has almost scarred Europe in a large measure, and chaos is the only word that explains the post-modern world. "The world is a fallen world; man is a fallen creature."(G. S. Frazer.) The uprooting of spiritual life and the futility of science have imprisoned us in the snares of greed and anger. Eliot's lament about spiritual drought in the blighted wasteland is true even in 2002:

> To Carthage then I came
>
> Burning burning burning burning
>
> O Lord Thou pluckest me out
>
> O Lord thou pluckest
>
> Burning

> (*Collected Poems*: 1909-1962, P.64.)

The state of rainlessness does not subside in the new millennium:

> Here is no water but only rock
>
> Rock and no water and the sandy road

> (P. 66.)

The tortuous imagery and the broken sentences in some poems of *The Golden Wings* reflect the troubled psyche of the author, and yet reveal an exuberant poetic fervor. They are not "random explosions" due to disintegration in society; on the other hand, they are enlivened by a sharp intelligence, attractive symbols, evocative rhythms and sumptuous imagery. Many poets in *The Golden Wings* may be compared with W. H. Auden, Stephen Spender, Cecil Day Lewis and Louis MacNeice, "the four musketeers of the Oxford Movement" in twentieth century English poetry. This is due to their cynicism and satire. "They came to feel as if they belonged to nowhere. A sense of the loss of moorings, of rootlessness, and a quest for a new base characterized the Oxford poets." A. C. Ward aptly comments that a thin whimper displaced both the song of joy and the strong cry of agony. Some poets of *The Golden Wings* reveal neo-romantic tendencies and seem to be influenced by poets like Dylan Thomas and George Barker, due to evocative and over-complex imagery. Some other poets in the anthology seem to be influenced by New Empsonians like John Wain, John Holloway, Donald Davie, Philip Larkin, Kingsley Amis, Thomas Gunn, Robert Conquest and Elizabeth Jennings, who "sought rather to construct than to pour themselves out in lamentations."

Besides, the American poets included in *The Golden Wings* reveal a capacity to see and to feel what life is. Moreover, their poems are marked by artistic workmanship. Some of the poems present a rare sense of the consummate artist. It is difficult to agree with the comment made by Andre Malraux that American literature is the only contemporary literature not written by intellectuals.

Sharon W. Flynn's "Spirit Flute Unending" reveals an accent of grave sweetness:

> My Sweet One,
>
> hear the sultry strains
>
> of my spirit flute...

The phrase "spirit flute" shows the poets' true poetic stature. Jan Oskar Hansen in his aerially imaginative poem "A Romance Remembered" remembers a woman he loved once. The poet is able to sustain his flight at his highest pitch:

> Now that I shall not see her again,
>
> too many years have dripped and
>
> made tiny holes on the sandstone
>
> of time, only the faint echo of her
>
> whispering voice remains:
>
> "Forever, forever my love."

Ikeda's "Summer And Winter" is a masterpiece of vivid and accurate description. The opening stanza is remarkable due to the detailed and matter-of-fact delineation of summer:

> The floating clouds in summer seem to be burning.
>
> Tormented by the sunlight dazzling and severe,
>
> The blades of grass gasp for breath, with great suffering.
>
> They wait the coming autumn, cool, bracing and clear.

One of the essential things about Ikeda is that he is one of the greatest poets of nature.

"The Banner" by Beatrice O'Brien is a deep, subjective, psychological analysis of the soldier's psyche. The "assisting nurse" probing the soldier's wound says:

> He ran into enemy fire
>
> to save the flag his buddy
>
> had raised, just yesterday.

After reading such lines one is halted to take a peep into the soldier's consciousness. "Observations From Oceanside, California" by Kirby Wright is full of inner and outer music. We find a spontaneous growth of poetic impulse in the following lines:

> A jogger appears
>
> then disappears
>
> into a mirage

"Utopia Is Not Too Far" by Amos Taiwo is a passionate indictment of accumulation of "wealth" without "hardwork" and "enlightenment":

> Enough of everything with wishes fulfilled
>
> Make room for bad economy.
>
> Not until adequate enlightenment passes round
>
> That wealth without matching hardwork cannot be sustained;

The idea of the poem is that man can come out triumphant out of chaos, if he strives to be guided by the light of his own soul. F. William Broome's "A Single Orange" is dominated by "fresh tartness found only in a single orange." The poet reveals poetic quality even in a commonplace subject. Due to a new type of theme, Broome finds the change in poetic technique inevitable:

> Coveted by all for exquisite taste
>
> its pungent aroma and singular flavor

filling a universal craving to taste
the juicy pulp of a single orange.

Deborah Ferber's "Spring Creations" is full of a beautiful sense of rhythm. The poetic style is evocative and suggestive: "Springtime love has no demands."

Barbara Hardcastle's "Wonder Fills My Heart" is sonorous and romantic. An exotic character of the imagery is concentrated in the following lines revealing combined magic and dignity:

Placidity encloses me,

from the vast, blue sky

to the splendor of the earth.

"You Are Beauty" by Lee Ennis is full of sweetness and harmonious melody, simplicity and naturalness. The poet has avoided all pomposities of thought and style:

When men speak of beauty they speak of you

You take my breath

You are beauty.

"Bengals" by Dr. Charles Albano is inspired by Bengalis "Guardians of royal splendor." The poem abounds in vivid word-pictures. Albano reveals the quality of a poet-painter:

The Bengal always strolls alone

Through Banyan-tangled building stone

Patrolling darkened corridors,

Corbeled vaults and marble floors

Brazos N. Mason's "Break Into Song" is full of transparent sincerity and the poet feels no unrest and despondency about death:

The way one goes

Does not matter

Shot by gun or

Crushed to splatter

The poet will "sing some songs", since "Life was much fun." This poem puts a very attractive face on darkness. The style of Geertruud Ida Maria's

"Unveiled Future" is one of exquisite finish. The poetic style reveals quite faultless phrases like "silk face", "mystique eyes", "diamond ears", "ruby soft lips". The poem ends with unsurpassable lines:

> Like the soft thin veil of a future bride
>
> Removed by the impatient groom
>
> Looking for tomorrows dowry.

Sudheesh V Nair's "Raindrops" is full of perfect melody. The majesty, the natural simplicity and vigor are evident:

> When the rain stops and the sun shines again
>
> I will start looking for my color in the sky

"I Would Like To Be Mad" by Giovanni Ghirga MD reveals a certain temperament and a way of looking at life. The poem is full of self-revelation and impressionistic style. The poet is interested in the complexities of human behavior. Giovanni Ghirga prefers madness and the lines assert this with consummate skill:

> I would like to be mad
>
> Not to understand the truth
>
> To dream by day
>
> And not to think looking.

"The Reality of Number Eight" by Shirley Bolstok is nearer to painting than music. The pictorial element is quite insistent, for example:

> *Seven strongholds* have brought him here
>
> I behold now, the trepidation of my fate
>
> He has conquered *seven hearts* before me
>
> He is the reality of *number eight*.

The poem is inspired by the Pre-Raphaelite Movement in English Poetry.

"World Of Dreams" by Lauren Diane Ovsevitz reveals the poet's pursuit of the unknown and the infinite. The poet dreams not for the limited happiness but for the illimitable joy:

> I wonder what its like to live in a World of Dreams
>
> where rain clouds are made of strawberry creams.
>
> Where lightening spreads gold all around.

The poem is full of the heroic struggle with reality. H. G. Brown's "The Listening Room" is penetrated, vitalized and made real by

> A place where foliage and music bloom
> In concert: wandering jew and succulent;
> Mozart, Miles, and spider plant.

To the poet, such a "concert" transcends the joys of ordinary mankind. The poem has an undeniable force and enlarges our conception of imaginative adventure.

Andrew's "Days In The Paradise of Grandma's House", Chelsea Comeau's "Perpetually This", Kato's "A Running Man", Yvonne Sparkes's "The Robin", Audrey A Cooper's "Our Marriage", Sean Nugent's "Nature's Gift", John Birkbeck's "Migratory Species", Venessa Aquilla Hall's "Chained Mind Detained", Sean David Gregson's "The Fog", Kathie Isaac-Luke's "Kinetics", Patricia Wellingham-Jones's "Choices", Anita Barrows' "Questo Muro", Alice Pero's "On Waiting For Creativity", Ginny Christiansen's "Fractured Fairytale", William James Jenkinson's "Emotional Rollercoaster" are full of music which goes straight to the heart . They reveal the clearness of vision and originality of mind. Poetry, says F. R. Leavis, "can communicate the actual quality of experience with a subtlety and precision unapproachable by any other means." The experiences, which the poets included in *The Golden Wings* express, reveal more than a temporary or local interest; they possess universality. Great poetry transcends geographical boundaries. "Our imaginations are but fragments of the universal imagination, and as we enlarge our imagination by imaginative sympathy, and transform, with the beauty and peace of art, the sorrows and joys of the world, we put off the limited mortal man more and more and put on the unlimited immortal man." (W.B. Yeats)

Allahabad
July 10, 2002

SANTOSH KUMAR

A

Adam Wang	13
Agnes Cowan	14
Alberto O Cappas	15
Alice Pero	17
Alisha Nicole Hubbard	18
Amos Taiwo	19
Andrea Venantius	21
Andrena Zawinski	23
Andrew	24
Andy Harding	25
Angeli'ca J. Varney	26
Ani Gjika	27
Anita Barrows	29
Annastasiya Alexandra	31
Annette Stone	32
Annie Finch	33
Arthur E. Holland Sr	34
Audrey A Cooper	35
Ayo Millers	36
Ayumi "Goldie" Kato	38

B

Balog Anna	39
Barbara Hardcastle	40
Beatrice O'Brien	41
Bertha Rose Young	42
Beth Grindstaff	43
Betty Hapgood	44
Birdie	45
Bitte Assarmo	47
Bogdan Tiganov	48
Brandon Miracle	49
Brazos N. Mason	51
Brent M. Parker	52

C

Carlos Hiraldo	54
Camilla E Clark	56
Chanda Witherspoon	57
Charles Albano	59
Charlotte Peters Rock	61
Chelsea Comeau	65
Chiesa Irwin	66
Christine A Kempster	67
Christopher R. Akins	68
Corrine De Winter	69
Cynthia Therese Hoffman	70

D

Damon D. Brewer	71
Dande Lampa Matusalem	72
Daniel William Gonzales	74
Darius Gabriel Bugarin	76
Dave Slater	77
David Hill	78
Deanna Dale Horton	79
Deborah FerBer	80
Deborah J. Norris	82
Deborah Russell	83
Debra Marie Reilly	84
Del Senkbeil	87
Dianne M. Sherwin	88
Dustin	89

E

Ed Zipek	90
Edith A. Jenkins	91
Elisha Porat	92
Elsy Satheesan	93

Emma Burgin	94
Elvira Selow	95
Eve Hall	96

F

F. William Broome	97
Filipe Miguel Gomes	100
Francis Figueroa	101
Frank Anthony	102
Fred Marmorstein	103

G

Gary Lehmann	104
Geraldine Sarmiento	106
Geertruud Ida Maria	107
Ginny Christiansen	109
Giovanni Ghirga MD	110
Goldie Mae	111
Gregory W Bryant	112

H

Harold Janzen	113
Heather La Croix	114
Heather Johnson	115
H. G. Brown	116
Hiram Larew	117
Howard Camner	118

I

Isadora SuZhen Snapp	119

J

Jack Conway	120
J. D. Nelson	122
Jan Oskar Hansen	123
Jason Clapham	126
Jason E. Windham	127
Jason McIntosh	128
Jessica Hatton	129
Jessie O'Donovan	133
Jill Chan	134
Joan Hambidge	135
John A Duffy	136
John Birkbeck	137
John Dempsey	139
John Michael Martinez	140
John Western	141
Joseph Aprile	142

K

Karen Alkalay-Gut	149
Kari Marie Gilbert	150
Kathie Isaac-Luke	151
Kathleen K. Harris	152
Kathleen Lawlor	153
Kathleen Rose Cruger	154
Kazuyosi Ikeda	155
Kenneth McManus	157
Kevin James Knowles	158
Kevin M. Horsley	160
Kimberly Beth Nelson	161
Kirby Wright	162
Kristine	163
Kristina Anna Lehner	164
Kuldeep Kaur	165

L

Larry Jaffe	166
Lauren Diane Ovsevitz	168
Len Rely	169
Les Wicks	170
LeVaughn Flynn	172
Lee R. Lowder III	173
Lee Ennis Lisa M. Lewis	174
Lisa M. Lewis	176
Lisa-Marie Griffin	177
Lowell Damron	178
Louise P. Saltkill	179
Lucretia Ann Campos	180
Luis Cabalquinto	181

M

Mandy Dyer	183
Marek Lugowski	184
Maria Cristina Azcona	185
Maria Theresa Ib	186
Marie	187
Marie Guay	189
Marki Twain	190
Martin A Enticknap	191
Mary Kathryn Cannon	192
Matthew Johnson	193
Melisande Luna	194
MercyRain	195
Michael D. Petti	196
Michael J Shepard	197
Michael Levy	199
Michael R. Collings	200
Michael Paul Chmielecki	202

Michelle Dunk-Martin	203
Mike Subritzky	204
Mukunda Tom Stiles	205

N

Natasha C. Burroughs	206
Nguyen Duc Batngan	207
Nicholas Gallimore	208
NIlanshu Kumar Agrawal	209

O

Olaf Korder	210
Olukoga Tayo	211

P

Padmore Agbemabiese	212
Page Malbrough	214
Pat Phillips West	215
Patricia Gomes	216
Patricia H. Regensburg	217
Patricia Wellingham-Jones	218

R

R.A.Munoz	221
Richard James Allen	222
Richard Paul Crowther	223
Richard Stevenson	224
Rickey K. Hood	226
Rina Ferrarelli	228
Robert Edgar Burns	229
Robert L. Jackson	231
Rodney Kuhn	232

Roland Leach	233		**T**	
Rolland G. Smith	235			
Romus Simpson	236		Taylor Graham	271
Ron Cole	237		Thelma Shutters	272
Rosa M. DelVecchio	239		Thomas Fortenberry	273
Ross Conrad Galvan	240		Timothy McNeal	274
Rune Leknes	241		Tina K Campbell	275
Ruth Daigon	242		Todd Burge	276
			Tony Bush	278
S			Tony Weaver	279
			Torey Fraley	281
Saaleha Bamjee	243		Troels Hundtofte	282
Salvatore Amico M. Buttaci	244			
Santosh Kumar	245		**U**	
Sean David Gregson	246			
Sean Nugent	247		Uppalapati Lakshmi Prasanthi	283
Serge van Duijnhoven	249			
Shabnam Abdoola	251		**V**	
Shalini Nayar	252			
Sharon W. Flynn	253		Venessa Aquilla Hall	285
Shawnte Orion	255			
Sherri Anderson	256		**W**	
Sheryl Mackiernan	257			
Shirley Bolstok	258		W. S. Mayo	286
Shivendra N Green	261		Ward Kelley	287
Sonia Edwards	262		William Dean Hamilton	289
Stanislaus Jaworski	263		William James Jenkinson	290
Steve Murray	264			
Steven Valentine	265		**Y**	
Stuart Jason Deutsch	266			
Sudheesh V Nair	267		Yvonne Sparkes	292
Susan K. Rowse	268			
Susie Davies	270		**Notes on Contributors**	293

Adam Wang

ETERNAL ABYSS

Monarch of Chaos I roam the planes,
Born from caverns of old earth,
A maelstrom of swirling flames surrounds my body,
As Darkness shields my wake,
Sorrow enters my sword's veins,
This entity lays waste to all who rebel,
Great armies I overwhelm,
Brilliant minds tip to madness,
Splendid societies collapse from my quakes,
What am I? So you inquire,
I am the eternal darkness that follows mankind.

Agnes Cowan

BUTTERFLY WITH SORE FEET

Walk gently, Life, for mortal souls are fragile,
Bent or broken by the trip may be;
Tread as a butterfly whose feet are wounded,
Unlike the feet of clay assigned to me
Whose gait is heavy, prone to constant falter
Each time some thorn in flesh impedes my feet;
Remove the pebbles that I shall not stumble,
Nor let the journey deal my heart defeat.

I pray for wings, as butterflies can travel,
To lift me to new heights each day I live,
And keep me, pray, forever full reminded
Of any service I was born to give.

My compass be not molded of rich metal,
But formed of love, my guiding instrument,
And any footsteps left in sand behind me,
Be clear intentions of my heart's intent.

Alberto O Cappas

THE PLEDGE
(Dedicated to our Children and Youth)

I pledge to maintain
A healthy mind and body,
staying away from the evil of drugs.
I pledge always to try my best to understand
the importance of knowledge and education,
painting a positive picture of where
I plan to be tomorrow,
not allowing obstacles to stop the growth
of my plans for the future.
I pledge to seek answers to questions,
understanding that the answers to questions
sometimes lead to other discoveries.
I pledge to work hard,
ith the awareness and confidence
that hard work today will serve
as the seeds for my strong tree tomorrow,
a tree no one will ever be able to tear down.
I pledge to learn proper languages,
beginning with my mother tongue,
always prepared to appreciate others.
I pledge to gain a better understanding of myself,
by understanding my cultural roots,

to fully accept who I am as a human being,
a rainbow of many cultures and colors.

I pledge to overcome any personal misfortunes,
always striving to become
A wiser person.

Alice Pero

ON WAITING FOR CREATIVITY

When the roots of my hair develop ears
and some strange unfeeling nodules in my outer crust,
(or is it inner?) turn the prescribed color,
then will I begin to create?
In a sudden spell or fit of consciousness
or during the lull in an invisible storm
will the pen begin to move across the page
of its own volition?
Struck full of speech by an asteroid that passed
during the right phase of the moon?
I am scientific. I have read discourses, papers and treatises.
The cells must congeal in the correct proportions.
I have fed myself, bone and blood, into a small vial
and discovered the contents.
Real, visceral.
Oh, speak to me through a glass tube and call to me
from an intricate maze, through the voice of rabbits!
I am waiting, and I am getting tired.
Maybe I could close my eyes and just be here.
But that would be too simple.

Alisha Nicole Hubbard

THE PAST

How can I live with out you in my life
I hope I never do
I hope you will always come to me when you have no one else to turn too.
I hope you realize how precious life is
I hope you understand how possible dreams can be
I hope you see how wrong she was for you and how right you are for me
I loved you a while it wasn't just lust
I hope you would see what you would miss
I can only give you now, not replace the past or predict the future
How will I live with out you in my life,
I hope all of your precious dreams come true.

GOOD-BYE

The sun will always shine in the east and set in my eyes,
Just like my love for you, It slowly dies.
You say it now so clearly,
You say you love me dearly
As it shines brightly,
I cant say this lightly
When it finally set's in my eyes, the sun
Then you know that I am done.

Amos Taiwo

THE LEGEND OF RIBOT

    'The legend of Ribot' was a story
A strange one told by the children of Freedom.
Ribot was the wanderer of Fair.
known to have been born in cheerlot,
He grew up in Lapotie, where he had a friend
whose name was called jolly parrot.
Jolly parrot was a handsome farmer in slumbernut.
Ribot and parrot enjoyed each other's company all the time.
Like one cold evening when they went on a horse riding adventure.
They rode to the town of Fury, but
Little did they know that, Fury was a place of the furies.
In order to trace the way to Downies,
They sought the path that led to Fury
Through which they came by some men of honor,
Those men were playing the game of 'Wonders in the Desert'.
Afterwards, Ribot and parrot made haste that cold evening
To find out the direction of the county of the Downies.
But the drunken men of Fury made jest of them and said,
'Downies is not only far away, but beyond your reach now'.
'Just keep on riding on for the next three days, you'll get there'.
Ribot and parrot spent all the time playing 'Wonders in the Desert'.
Since no one could give them clear direction of Downies, and
Neither of them was ready to get lost
while seeking the road to Downies,
The tired wanderers had no option but to rest for the night,
As the duo spent most of the night guessing and guessing
'which way? which way?, until they ran out of guesses.

UTOPIA IS NOT TOO FAR

Plenty today more plenty tomorrow
if wishes were horses beggars would ride
The best of them live well ever after
There are more than enough beggars
To go round the world of wants and needs.
But were it in a utopia
Too many lazy drones would spoil the fun;
Enough of everything with wishes fulfilled
Make room for bad economy.
Not until adequate enlightenment passes round
That wealth without matching hardwork cannot be sustained;
Ideal, it is, for coming generations to inherit a
state of total convenience
To make room for continued prosperity.
Where this is attainable
The forces of consumption and production are in harmony,
For good balance of our continued profitable existence; and so
Let the people thank their stars and praise their fortune;
For the god of plenty has smiled on them;
As long as they remain ready
To keep on working, and
To keep on producing, so that
They can keep on consuming
For a glorious hardworking people.

Andrea Venantius

HEAD HOLDING FEET

And so we stand
our hearts intertwined
with every glance,
but with feet
firmly apart,
and lips
following
stubborn feet.

TRAIN AT NIGHT

The train isn't
as fun at night,
when the windows
reflect
more of yourself
than any view
outside.
It's at best a time shuttle,
in realistic travel,
getting you
to your chosen
destination,
as expected.

I prefer landscape
lulling me to sleep,
rather than thoughts
designed to block out
the time traveled.

Andrena Zawinski

FROGS AT THE END OF MY PEN

    We are talking at the poets
    workshop about caesura and kicking
    Donald Hall's leaves, not in
    October or in New Hampshire
    with boots on. We're kicking leaves
    in clauses with stresses, and I'm missing
    something. I think of frogs
    in summer at the swimming hole
    in Meadville. I think fresh
    dissections, wonder where eggs are
    first or last, wonder if
    meaning jumps or slides
    through a form at the end
    of my surgical pen while I'm kicking
    these leaves, and I am still
    missing something. I hear
    frogs at the swimming hole
    in Meadville and night
    pregnant with sound.

Andrew

DAYS IN THE PARADISE OF GRANDMA'S HOUSE
(In memory of Muriel Jagger, God rest your soul, my beloved grandma)

The sun rises gently upon grandma's garden
Rays of light beam down on the roots of grass
I can hear the birds twittering amongst themselves
The serenity, the tranquillity, the peace that never lasts

Grandma calls, breakfast is ready
A morning spent idly watching television
In-between breaks we talk about grandma's memories of the past
Her childhood, marriage, children, the loss of her husband and other events
Stories of joy, sadness and her hopes for the future
To me it is a diet, of sorts, that is pure entertainment

This goes on for several days
Then its time to go home, to my parents
To fighting with my siblings for the remote
Driving my mum mad with my laconic habits
Worrying about my exam results that will shape my future
The normal, anarchistic existence of family life
Far away from the now heavenly delights
Of waking up to see grandma's divine 'Garden of Eden'

Andy Harding

A LOVE LIES BLEEDING

    The bitter words I heard tonight
    Ran round my head, my chest felt tight
    A dagger plunged deep in my heart
    When did this deception start?
    A love so special, you've destroyed
    I'm too distraught to be annoyed
    How could you act so deviously
    Not taking love so seriously
    My heart left damaged, out on the floor
    As you left, you closed the door
    You didn't listen to my pleading
    Now you're gone, a love lies bleeding.

Angeli'ca J. Varney

PERFECT DREAM

I have stolen a glimpse of you,
taken you into my world,
welcomed you into my dreams.
Following me,
unwitting of where you were going,
I pulled you further with me,
deeper into my being,
and I draped you in my love.
Helpless to save yourself,
you found your were clinging to me,
and loving me increasingly,
with each day passing.
In my intense dreams,
we held and touched,
and I was finally able,
to kiss your lips,
taste your essence,
sweet upon my tongue.
With every touch,
every caress of your fingertips,
every nerve in my body,
came alive,
begging for a chance,
a single moment to feel you.
Every movement was perfect,
every sensation just right.
You were my perfect dream,
 my brightest star in the sky,
and you restored my passion.

Ani Gjika

A LESSON IN TONGUES

    my lover wants me
    to teach him languages
    so i sit him with me by the trees
    and thus begin...
    i will teach you poli linguas
    all the linguas that you thelis,
    thelis like they say in greek
    when they want something,
    TH as in "Thighs"
    these of mine i wrap around
    your waist just so;
    and E as in "bEd"
    this grassy bed we lie in;
    L as in "Labials"
    the sounds coming through
    these lips when i speak to you
    in tongues, then kiss
    you uuhhmmm and uuhmm;
    and I as in "frIction"
    what you feel when my hand
    crawls your body over
    like so and like so and finally
    S as in "suSurrous"
    when my mouth comes to your ear
    and says, "i lohh it whe you shhh like blu
    hhhusssssshhhpurrreessssaabeeeaamm"
    Thelis, tell me che tu thelis

and i give, i say.
but you will have to be silenzioso
when i ablo, i say,
and listen soltanto a me,
that means you have to listen
very attentivement, looking at
my mouth, le mie labbra especially
and when i tell you, love,
répéter after moi,
you will répéter so perfettamente,
deliciosissimo as you are
that i will say bravo,
bravo mon dieu, i would even call you
by such name, i would, you, god of my words.
and then i would speak albanian,
which in albanian is "shqip"
as in "schkeep" and you would say
shqip is the mejor lengua, ma belle,
the most bukur "bookoor"
beautiful, beautiful
and vuala! it will make
your thoughts grow red,
redder, like the russian blood,
krassneei blood and last, il culminacion
de my teaching sará when i tell you
to shut up now, non répéter anymore,
just tell me, in what language
will you now describe my eyes?

Anita Barrows

QUESTO MURO

You will come at a turning of the trail
to a wall of flame
After the hard climb & the exhausted dreaming

you will come to a place where he
with whom you have walked this far
will stop, will stand

beside you on the treacherous steep path
& stare as you shiver at the moving wall, the flame

that blocks your vision of what
comes after. And that one
who you thought would accompany you always,

who held your face
tenderly a little while in his hands —
who pressed the palms of his hands into drenched grass
& washed from your cheeks the soot, the tear-tracks —

he is telling you now
that all that stands between you
& everything you have known since the beginning

is this: this wall. Between yourself
& the beloved, between yourself & your joy,

the riverbank swaying with wildflowers, the shaft
of sunlight on the rock, the song.
Will you pass through it now, will you let it consume

whatever solidness this is
you call your life, & send
you out, a tremor of heat,

a radiance, a changed
flickering thing?

Annastasiya Alexandra

NAKED

Swarms of confusion
Delusions and conclusions
Love
Madness and latency
Love
Coffee binges, juices of emotions
Sneaks of happiness
Visions of bodies in an embrace
Not being able to touch you
Sinister actions
Saintly reactions
Minds filled with concepts
Terminology I can't understand
I can't reach my orgasm
I can't corrupt my bubble of trust
Cycle of rhythm
My postpartum sadness
My fear of me leaving
Your face diluted by those who have slept in the same bed
Visions are fast
Drive one wild with imagination
Imagination, you unleashed
Took off its hinges, ripped off the boards
Then I am naked
With out my feelings
Naked
Covered by images, splashes of imagination.

Annette Stone

A LITTLE DAILY PRAYER

Dear God this I hope, I pray.
That you will meet our needs for today.
What is held by tomorrow only you know.
So help us God as we go.
Give us the patience to meet each trial.
Remind us our troubles are only for a wile.
Give us the will to help and forgive each other.
Remind us that we should all love one another.
Comfort us please when we are sad.
Remain with us through the good and bad.
For there is no other God but you.
And we give you praise and thanks for all that you do.

Annie Finch

RUNNING IN CHURCH
for Marie

>Then, you were a hot-thinking, thin-lidded tinderbox.
>Losing your balance meant nothing at all. You would
>pour through the aisles in the highest cathedrals,
>careening deftly as patriarchs brooded.
>
>You made the long corridors ring, tintinnabular
>echoes exploring the pounded cold floor,
>forcing the walls to the truth of your progress:
>there was a person in this church's core.
>
>Past thick stained-glass colors wafted and swirling
>in pooled interludes that swung down from the rafters,
>cinnabar wounds threw light on your face, where the
>pliant young bones were dissolving in laughter.

Arthur E. Holland Sr

I ASKED TO BE BORN...

I petitioned heaven, I wanted to be a three dimensional creature,
I wanted to be black like the night of a million stars,
I asked for a body- and you gave me this...
It was able to withstand the storms,
It could survive the sun, and though man would strike it,
It remained resilient,
I asked for wisdom and the wherewithal to preserve it.
I built the pyramids to edify it. I asked to be born...
I sought the secrets of success, I did not add color to it,
nor did I alter the melanin therein.
I watched it shine like the oil of the earth,
I gave it labor, I gave it love, You gave it life!
I performed my mission,
I multiplied, the soil became my mother
to whom I must return this gift.
Yes this gift to be born.
Manifested spirit, magnified molecules,
metaphorical madness, edified existence.
Not a tree or a rock nor vegetation,
unable to fly now.
I acquiesce,
The tropical waters reflect my being,
the echoes whisper: "Granted"
I asked to be a man.
And here I stand.
Born!

Audrey A Cooper

OUR MARRIAGE

Our Marriage withstood time, and through the
years, time took its toll on our relationship.
Sometimes with more benefit's than most.
We had our share of troubles, ups and downs.
Raising our children, even though we didn't
know how. There came changes in our relationship,
sharing triumphs, failures, and your successes.
There were times, I regarded you as my confidante
And best friend too. I told you things, asked your
advice and sought your opinion on so many things
that I could not tell no other.

Our years together have been many, sharing,
counseling, helping, arguing with each other about
so many things. Sometimes, I think we have
had more good than bad in our relationship.
We are becoming older, getting stronger from
year-to-year and decade-to-decade. And as
time evolves, goes on, if we are no longer
together you will always have a place in my
heart, and be my best friend!

Ayo Millers

A VILLAGE GIRL

A bundle of grass on her head
she came, her hips swinging
Full like wine pitchers
She, the girl from my village

Pataki and mustard flowers
Like blue and yellow eyes
peep through the green grass

Long blades of grass
Hang over her eyes
Like green tassels
A net of green dreams
Her face caught in it

She left her skirt up to her knees
And holds my arm to cross the Suhan River
Ankle-deep water rises to her knees, to her waist,
Her legs disappear beneath the shimmering water,
And her skirt goes up like an upturned umbrella

The water goes down her thighs, her knees, her ankles,
so does her skirt,
'Thank you, brother', she says
Like a koel cooing from a mango grove
And leaves my arm and goes away

On the sand hill her footprints
Gleam like a prisoner's chain

She goes up the mound
Tall and slim like a sugar cane
And becomes a part of the green tree

She did not look at me
I could not see her face caught in the green net
But I cannot shake off
The dust of her touch.

Ayumi "Goldie" Kato

A RUNNING MAN

A man
passes running
on the bridge ... not noticing
a lot of swings he has left
up down.

Balog Anna

I GAVE MY LOVE TO YOU

I loved you once,
a long time ago
Now I'm just sorry that you are gone
Take my tears,
hold them to you
and remember that you were loved
Hear my laughter
Hear my cry,
remember me like I was before
When I gave you my heart you gave me silence
I loved you once but now you are gone...

Barbara Hardcastle

WONDER FILLS MY HEART

"Wonder Fills My Heart"
At the edge of the cliff, I stand,
arms extended up and out,
head slightly tilt back,
as the ocean's whitecapped waves
roll in and bang against the rocks.
Placidity encloses me,
from the vast, blue sky
to the splendor of the earth.
A world that wobbles with
perplexities and sensory delights.
I inhale the redolent sea,
as the gentle breeze
sweeps against my skin
with its warmth.
I was profoundly inspired,
while I listened to the distinct sounds
of the outdoors.
A mental spa was created,
with nature's vivid images and peace.
Patiently and affectionately, I cradled it.
A meditation of awe that soothes.

Beatrice O'Brien

THE BANNER

The soldier's lips were blue
Skin pale, white as this page.
Intravenous tubing
ran, blood red, into a vein.
an assisting nurse spoke
as the weary surgeon
probed the jagged wound,
"He ran into enemy fire
to save the flag his buddy
had raised, just yesterday."
Tears fell on a sterile field.

That night we all stood
in silence, saluting
a flag-draped boy...on his
long journey home.

Bertha Rose Young

TACO BELL AND SMOKEY

My name is baby I am adopted and love my parents very much;
But they wanted me to have a brother;
So they brought this skinny little dude home for me to play with;
Well he does not no the meaning of rest and relaxing;
Every time I get laid out for a nap here he comes;
Nipping at my nose if I hide it under the cover he goes for my heals;
I wish somebody had ask me before they got him
because my days are not looking to good unless
I can figure out how to get rid of him;
But if I did mom would just cry;
So guess I will just keep him and;
Figure how I can get him to gain weight like me;
Then he will slow down;
If you guys have any good ideas let me know.

Beth Grindstaff

WINTER

The leaves were already turning
When the children went back to school
And I could already feel the orange light of autumn
Lulling me to sleep
After that nervous summer insomnia.
I watched the birds
Pulling out in droves,
Leaving a few stragglers behind to fend for themselves.
And off the flapping wings of a raven
I could taste the cool scent of rain.
I'd sit alone in our room
While the air outside tightened and turned.
And maybe I'd read a book
While the sky darkened my heart a little more.
I'd listen to your breathing
In the desperate silence that comes just before the first snow,
And I'd wonder how much longer you could go
Before you'd pull the hammer back and fade away
Into a silence only I could hear.
Do you remember that day in August?
When we sat in my car by the lake?
I listened to the soft rolling thunder drown out your silence
And I tried to ignore the cold emptiness in my heart.
I knew then that you were already gone.
That I was here.
Alone.

Betty Hapgood

YE GODS, MY BOOKSHELF'S TOO BLOODY NOISY

One of the books on my shelf rang
It was 'The Primal Scream'
So I answered the book
'AAAAAAARGH !!!' it said
One of my other books
Vibrated along the shelf
It was 'The AA book of the Road'
I answered it
And got run over

All the books began to ring at the same time
The ring got louder and louder
I didn't want to answer 'Poisonous Spiders of South America'
Or 'The Dictionary of Icelandic Swearwords
and General Abuse in Suits'
I already told Naomi Campbell's autobiography that I'm engaged
So I decided to speak to 'The Tale of Two Cities'
I said 'Why two cities can't just leave me alone, Lord of the Rings
only knows'
'Trout Fishing in America' by Richard Brautigan is about fishing in
America, for trout, It said 'maggots, twine, and plenty of time, is the key'

I was in a Catch-22 Headlock, Sherlock Holmes where are you? Here
comes the end-If you blink you'll missit Did you blink?

Birdie

FAMILY PICNIC!

Picnic, row boats, river bank flows
Oars, paddles, whistles blow
Parasols, give a little shade
Blankets on the ground are laid
Sack cloth races, down a hill
Can watch it all from ferris wheel
Horse shoes, blue ribbon, apple pies
Some winner's laughed
Some winner cried
Cherry pie aroma.....made you grin,
To stuff yourself
Was an awful sin,
Seed spitting contest came up next,
Sticky, gooey, out right mess !
Catching butterflies,
Letting them go,
Reach for bumblebee
Momma shrieks, " No !"
Clinging to tire
Swinging high from tree
Then jump in river,
On count of three

BOUQUETED FLOWER FIELD'S

Walking through meadows
Bouqueted flower fields
There's daisies, dandelions
Sweet daffodils

Yellow, white
Red roses too
Carnations, bluebonnets
Gladiolas sprout bloom

Beautiful violets
Blushing with pride
Perky sunflowers
Kissing blue skies

Close your eyes tight
Until no light
Dream , dream

Dream!

You'll find
Bouqueted
Flowered fields
Beyond life's rippling streams.

Bitte Assarmo

VOICE FROM HIDDEN ROOMS

    Broken voice
    Calling my name
    No one hears
    No one sees
    but you can scent the wind in your hair
    And you see the world from hidden rooms
    Perhaps you are free
    your meaningful life
    With broken voice
    For eternity.

COLOURFUL

    For many years you were there
    Full of colours, full of grace
    Like a bird in the sky
    always free
    but in the end you were always returning to me

    Now you're gone
    like the wind you can no longer be seen
    But I feel you
    Next to me
    Always.

Bogdan Tiganov

LATE AT NIGHT

He burst upon me
at quarter past three
I thought it was morning
with his beard and sunglasses

The bomb went off
the toxins came down
acids burnt my tongue
everybody shares a feeling

I was in the desert
and it was polar bear cold
He slammed the simple door
and it surprised me damn it.

Brandon Miracle

TO HAVE BEEN

Autumn leaves fall all around,
swirling and drifting in directions
that never existed before tonight.
and I know what you are
is sure to be pure. surely!
so why do I pick now to lose that sight?

why now, of all times,
with beauty spinning,
never stopping the constant flowing
of a steadfast river, with its white waves
clashing against rocks, who have seen paragon,
and turned up their stone chins to it?
with beauty fast sleeping
under the sky, which had recently been snowing
upon ground not hardened, but softened
by the white-winter years we wished had gone,
but returned to greet and grin. we submit.

but the white in the falling snow
and the white waves that give a river its glow
cannot compare to the contrasting colours
of the twisting leaves,
of an autumn eve.
of course, this, the beauty of all creation,
pales in comparison to you,

the holder of beauty of no boundaries, no foundation.
your beauty is feral, unconstrained.

to know of autumn's beauty is to have seen,
to know of loving you is to have been.

Brazos N. Mason

BREAK INTO SONG

    Break into song
    When I've passed
    Does not matter
    I'm sliced or gassed

    Or lost my breath
    In sand so quick
    Or beat to death
    By pointy stick

    By truck wheels high
    I'm run over
    Or crossed by plow
    In field of clover

    The way one goes
    Does not matter
    Shot by gun or
    Crushed to splatter

    So, sing some songs
    Life was much fun
    Joy for me, it's
    Over and done!

Brent M. Parker

HEAVEN'S HELLDOG

Life's a finely detailed heaven
Guarded by a versatile Cherubs

One head to drool a gelatinous moat
Around you
As it sniffs the wafting scents from Tomorrow
One head to know on the bones of Yesterday
And the head head
Licks this moment
Appetizing itself
As you stare.

Three such heads, you could handle, but
Three such, you've chained
To guard each explorable facet
For unleashed, you think, they'd bring chaos
Leaping in your lap at the unexpected
And you'd have to take down your "Beware of Dog" signs.

Each mouth,
With it's own uniquely sculpted teeth
Clamped in ancient bites.

Each brain
Devising devious new ones.

Necks connectingm
In a bloated black body
Jiggling with unstilled
Fear.

Carlos Hiraldo

BACK IN THE DR

From the deep
deep slumber
of the Anglo-Saxon,
I'm born again.

In a twin GE
power burst,
I'm black
to save the Universe...

or ¾ of a Caribbean
Island...

or my disparate family...

Perhaps. I should just
look in the mirror
and learn to smile
before the inevitable
black out.

90 degrees
of heat and humidity.
Like dew
from the Presidente bottle,
sweat dripped

from my forehead
before I entered
my air-conditioned splendor.

El Bar de la Esquina,
like on any street corner of the world,
Irish, black, the poor, the oppressed
everything in me
comes to rest here.

I drink up
before the violence starts,
so it may seem natural
to me.

Camilla E Clark

SONNET FOR MY BELOVED MGT

I look in bewildered awe and envious aspiration
At the poetry of others and the beauty held within,
But yet when I attempt to create that of my admiration,
My words appear weak, pretentious and thin.
They cannot compare with my emotion,
They cannot reflect my feelings,
They cannot show my devotion,
Nor the music my heart sings.
The sweet sonnets of others are perfection,
My humble attempt does not match,
Yet still I write with these thoughts and affection
Which to conclude, for you I will attach:
Although my crude words cannot compare with my love so true,
All that matters is that my love is you.

Chanda Witherspoon

A DREAM OF DESTINY

Closing my eyes tonight, and
I have no idea what is going to occur.
The lights go out and so does my darkness.
The roses have lost its scent,
but my skin smells of its lent.
I want to become everything sensual;
I want to be everything seductive.
I want to be a disappearing act.
White sand is on my bedroom floor.
Candles dangling from my ceiling.
The moon is sitting right next to my window,
gazing at me laying on my bed,
as oil is some how poured down my spin.
A sensational feeling comes over my body
as the oil sinks deep into my heart, reaching my soul.
I flash back to a time when the sky was orange
and the ocean was lavender.
The air smelled of coconut,
and the people did not have human forms,
but were merely souls.
What an intimate feeling that could not escape my lungs.
So I took short deep breaths,
panting a prayer that sooth my soul.
I floated back to my room where the air was cool.
I suddenly found myself underneath my bed,
which changed into the ocean.

I held my breath afraid that if
I inhaled I would surely drown.
What could I possibly do but take a chance.
As I opened my mouth water started filling my lungs,
I almost panicked.
That's when I realized I could breath underwater,
and that's when I realized that I could breath underwater.
I noticed several different objects moving towards me,
and a cautious manner.
Speaking to one another in a squealing voice,
that I soon understood.
They said to one another "Is it she?"
It couldn't possible be the Goddess of Love.
As they got closer there forms began to become clear.
For amongst me where Sharks, Dolphins, Octopuses,
Whales, Eels, and many other sea creatures circling around me
singing praises to the all-great Goddess of Love.
We were one in harmony, our energy was one in love,
our beings, were one in peace,
and our love was one in eternity.
As I opened my eyes from my night's encounter,
unable to move, unable to speak, unable to think,
I felt something go !
inside my soul and transform my dysfunctional emotions.
Was this a dream? Was this a vision?
What was I experiencing?
I decided what ever it was,
that I would just let go.
I would just let go and become that Goddess of Love
that I was perceived to be by the creatures of the sea.
As I close eyes tonight, I will be free.
I will open myself up to a world that can only be reached by me.

Charles Albano

BENGALS

Afoot on endless paces,
They guard the sacred places—
Their trails mark long migrations
Throughout the jungle nations
Where those fearsome predators
Stalk crumbled walls on padded paws.

Where monuments to gods and kings
Since golden ages stand and sing
Of pious heavens built on earth
Assuring man of true rebirth—
There the Bengals make their home.

They laze atop sandstone spires,
Prowl long-extinguished holy fires,
Fallen palaces and fountains,
All alike, their sacred mountains.

Like columns left there face to face
Vying for the tallest place
In ancient cities overgrown
Unchallenged Bengals stand-alone.

The Bengal always strolls alone
Through Banyan-tangled building stone
Patrolling darkened corridors,
Corbeled vaults and marble floors,

As if in doing to imbue,
In deadened chambers, life anew.

Guardians of royal splendor,
Are your glances meant to render
Resplendent figures lasting peace
In Jamun groves where all cares cease?

Charlotte Peters Rock

DESTROYING HISTORY IN TILLYA TEPE

Along the Silk Route Tillya Tepe
hid a Bactrian treasure burial
Treasure with the bones they found there

Archaeologists and workers
patient brushing every feature
logging every smallest placement

Ancient bodies spoke of riches
Golden crowns and golden hair-pins
dressed them for a golden future

One young woman wore a fire crown
A nomad's crown of golden life trees
made to flatten to her saddle

Another woman wore a necklace
hollow gold and ivory beadwork
fine and varied for her honor

Every grave site told a story
Styles of Scythia and Greece
mingled India as Kushan

A mound above the fire temple
resting through an ancient village
carried bodies fine and noble

A warrior with his sword and dagger
dressed in silk and golden baubles
Nomad horse to guard his resting

They plotted out and cleaned the goldwork
photographed and worked the levels
sent it on to Kabul City

Then the war swept in and over
turquoise studded bears and buckles
golden Scythian warrior horsemen

Looting soldiers took the treasures
opened graves in Tillya Tepe
sold their golden-magic future

Here they offered work for money
history from two millennia
spread as nothing more than gold-weight
-
After they were driven outwards
archaeologists and workers
told remembered tales forever
-
Women buried in the fire-halls
in a thousand years of temple
through the village crumbled after

One was thirty - maybe forty
One was sixteen at her dying
One was young in plainest costume

But Oh her finest collar necklace
- drops of garnet mixed with turquoise
set in finest gold - was with her

Another - and the first we found there -
dressed in tiny plates of gold-ware
pointed where the others rested

One - a princess so we thought her -
with her pendent Aphrodite
winged in high design of Bactria

with an Indian mark of marriage
on its forehead for her pleasure -
dressed in spangled golden platelets

And her crown was tall in splendor
hung in drops of leaves and circles
set with turquoise-centred flowers

Shapes of hearts and moons and tree-like
made to lie in silent saddle
as the nomad trail moved onward

Only one men found a place there
He a warrior with his waist band -
nine gold Goddesses on lions -

gone to meet his long remaining
meet his Afterlife in splendor
where the Gods would claim his kinship

After all the finds were gathered -
as the war raged through the Afghans -
rain and falls disclosed the others -

Two more grave sites - bones and goldware
Who was buried in these coffins
no one searches to discover

But the gold was sold forever
into penury-collections
hoarded nameless out of culture

Archaeologists and workers
hear the vaguest news of battles
hear the news of auctioned goldware

Still their dreams pick round the grave-sites
lost forever in the carnage
high along the Afghan frontier.

Chelsea Comeau

PERPETUALLY THIS

O! From whence, I do beg, did this wretchedness rise,
Swelling like crescendos from poignant violins?
-When this, the winter of discontent is nigh,
All existence is dry. And from below, a collaboration of sins,

A verity brought forth from the yawning abyss,
Erupting, much like a scream, with a flickering gale.
Calamity is no longer a stranger! Life is amiss!
Dearest one, thy flesh has grown pale.

These whispers you shout are most plaguing! Obscene!
O! Wounded heart, thy mutiny is most cruel!
And yet, there she lies, slumbering softly.

And so I implore, though you surge into gloom
Where dark choirs of arch angels do sing of thy doom,
Fear not... for these defamations are all that we have.

Chiesa Irwin

OCHRE

    Standing on the ochre earth
    the woman dreams of mountains
    under a shroud of snow
    slashed with frozen falls
    brushed upon blue palette
    like mist from a god's mouth
    who with another hand
    threw ideas of stone and dirt
    ignited by his eyes
    into the ochre earth
    calling the herd around her
    she questions the creating mind
    that played with heat and sand
    and made her a spot
    where jostling animals
    vie for her shadow space.

Christine A Kempster

A PRAYER FOR LIFE

The Lord has wisdom; He has wonder in His name
He bestows His love as life and He gives us all our measure
Jesus his son was sent to pronounce his boundless love
To teach us the way, To reach the Father one day
We only have to open our hearts and
Listen to that voice therein

He placed His love deep within before the moment of birth
And retrieves it later at the moment of final release

When He deems it right, His love in our hearts
Will shine out and point the way, Heaven is the goal
We are born with love deep inside; we die with it still strong
Love returns to love and God in His infinite wisdom always collects His dues
The love buried deep within us surfaces and is drawn back towards the source

The source is God
The messenger is Jesus
The last journey we ever make is HOME !!

Christopher R. Akins

FUTURE EX-BOYFRIEND

Wouldn't it be funny - You could be my future ex-boyfriend.
Now, let's envision - how might that go?
Dramatic scenes unfurling in the car, yeah - in the parking lot,
Cheating a plenty, the slaughtering of friendship -
Measured in moments - We would put on the most tragic of shows.

I could be your prince, and you'd be my pauper.
How fundamentally strange that would seem;
Swimming in ticket stubs of foreign movies,
Sharing unclothed antics - Stitching up all our open dreams.

And, you just might be my future ex-boyfriend.
Even with the lights on, I can see that.
Dramatic, post-romantic, pedantic and stumbling
straight from attraction into - my God, what was that?

Okay..it might be lovely;
To have a love affair, that stresses the love.
The only question, my beautiful friend,
Could it ever be so - Could it ever become?
Push me into romantic - Pull me into your bed.
Let go this - Unfolded tension.
Let's say things that we've never said.

Yeah, it would be funny - You - My future ex-boyfriend.
But when this thing implodes, who's shoulder will catch my tears?
Shattered Angel, where would I go then? it's clear as chaos.

Yet, oh - somehow - We kiss - We begin this.
How crazy sensual. How lovely absurd.

Corrine De Winter

HAIKU

The bright Japanese lilies
Short of breath
In the summer afternoon.
What a rapid life ours is,
To bloom and die
In another's room.

This is love
Something impossible
The color of blue
Thrown at us like daggers
In a circus show

The jukebox in my heart
Keeps playing you.

Cynthia Therese Hoffman

HOLD BACK MISTY NIGHT SKY!

Share your heart, tickle my sensations, inspire me!
Sounds of nothing, lonely night air,
Wandering to nowhere, longing for your love.
Mountain top near, sun setting to night,
Thirsting for your heart, wishing you to me.

Waiting for a sign, not a sound to be heard,
No magic awaits me, as night fills the sky.
Bring me the moon, cascade stars my way,
Shine light ever brightly, lead me to my love.

Moon dances with stars, illuminate night air,
Wind rolling past me, singing to the trees.
Head tilted skyward, one last hopeful cry,
Silence...quiet, as sorrow touches my cheek.

Night turns to dawn I awaken to hope,
Defeated, saddened heart heavy with pain,
Every breath hurts, release my heart aching,
Shed no more tears, HOLD BACK MISTY NIGHT SKY!

Damon D. Brewer

LOVE ME

    Love me tenderly—lovingly.
    I love you;
    Please love me.
    Love me tenderly—kindly.
    Please love me—
    The way that I love you.

Dande Lampa Matusalem

SAVANNA

Sun sets down,
to ask for another day.
a little girl kneels,
folds both hands and starts to PRAY.

Asking, "Dear LORD,
please bless my mommy, daddy and my best FRIEND.
Thank you so much,
for the three blessings that you send."

Various BLESSINGS,
she asked, and they whizzed through her head.
She thanked GOD for JESUS,
and for him being born like the ANGEL said.

"AMEN" she finished,
unfolded her hands and went to sleep,
she dreamed of 3 KINGS,
a manger, an ox, and a baby sheep.

Night came to an end,
the sun's wish was granted.
The little girl grew,
another SEED OF FAITH was planted.

Never was she lonely,
for every night she PRAYED.

and was she ever HAPPY,
for a FOREST OF FAITH she made.

"ALLELUIAH" she sang,
and with open HEART the LORD came in.
SAVANNA is her name,
And still ends her day with the word, 'AMEN'.

Daniel William Gonzales

HELEN PATRICIA SHORB
(MY GRANDMOTHER, THE SAINT!)

You may not hear of her in church
or see her face on cathedral walls
but Helen Patricia Shorb, my grandmother
was a saint among women!

She gave so much love, spread wells
of it to whoever she met
ask any of her students, they will tell you
of her brilliance. She was a scholarly
woman, she knew six languages and could
translate entire novels from Danish to English.

She may not have been rich or famous
but she had pen pals all across the world
She never missed a day of church
until the pain got to be too much
Even after she was diagnosed with cancer, never
did she stifle a smile of joy on her face
and the next time I saw her, she asked,
"How are you?"

She gave & gave & gave
and many of us feared that she left
nothing for herself
but that's just the way she was.

My mother told me of how
I would give her bruises on her shins
as a child because I would be so excited
to see her, I would race over in my baby
walked and slam into her legs.

I smile to think of her absolute sincerity
I always thought, "this is what an angel must be like"
I will never forget the last time I held her hand
for what seemed like eternity
and time seemed to stop briefly for a moment
and for the first time in my life
I felt I understood God.

Darius Gabriel Bugarin

ONE THING MORE

    I know —
    It's too long for you to wait
    But please be patient
    Sooner —
    You'll have what you want
    But I never promise
    As I'm observing you one more thing
    And if I see this to you today
    Maybe —
    I'll give you my love tomorrow.

Dave Slater

TEN ROOMS

In the back of the night between the limbs of deceit
I enter the rich hangings of the forest.
My bed cradles an ancient civilization of women
Crying on the sunken breasts of warriors;
Dust on lips where tongues should rest.

The tidal waves of spring push me weakly
Backwards to winter. Why are we concerned
With ancient myths of our origins?
Is it fear of the present or a prick of
Fear for the power of the past? Can we
Succumb once more, once more
To the consolation of the belly of the earth?
Or do we need the succour of modern lives
And the frenetic moments of the now?

Questions of being, of existence trouble
Few people, but the heart and the mind
Rest uneasy in all who travel
The pathways of these troubled times.
So continue with me and enter
The solitude of these ten resurgent rooms.

David Hill

WET SHAVE

    Get in
    At eight p.m. and someone's garbled message,
    Which may or may not be
    You, in an emergency,
    Is all it takes to have me slapping cream all round my chin,
    Wild for a marriage
    Of two soft swathes of shaven skin.

Deanna Dale Horton

DUSTY WATER FROM A STRANGER'S HANDS
-my thanks to Eric Lieberman

>At eighteen I was offered my first real drink,
>Not beer or wine
>But water-from a lone rusty pipe.
>
>In the shade of a dusty almond orchard,
>The heat of the California north valley
>Weakened me near fainting.
>I was barely capable of standing alone.
>
>Someone in the group found a spigot.
>Unable to hold my own hands together-
>A man I hardly knew
>Cupped his
>And I drank.

Dr. Deborah Ferber

SPRING CREATIONS

Oh spring time romance
Create the love we all desire
Flowers bloom with no remorse
Butterflies have no loves boundaries

Springtime love has no demands
Natures love spreads like seeds in wind
Each new seed creates new life
With every seed of life there is a bond
Spring bares the fruit of love of life

LIFE'S THORNY THISTLES

The thorny thistle,
Thumped my sky,
Thinking about the reasons why,
Thrusting through life's thistles,
Thanking those that helped me through,
The thorny thistles of life.

GREATNESS

New hope for all,
Rich and poor and minorities too,

Human rights and women's rights,
Road Scholar wanting to serve us all,
Secrets forgiven for past discretions,
Smart wife that had a life.

Balanced books and budgets cuts,
Foreign policy preventing genocide,
Markets up and interest rates are down,
Creating a better life for all.

Things were good but not enough,
Lust and lies opening our eyes,
Creating tears of disappointment,
Indiscretions claimed by others,
Should we claim a person fall?
Greatness should be measured,
Conviction,
Service,
Action,
Love for all.

Deborah J. Norris

WHISPER OF THE ROSE

Just knowing you are there,
Brightens my day...
I sit and wait to hear from you to see
What you have to say..
I hope you can find a Rose each day...
For if you can, put it to your ear....
You will hear....
My voice each day...

Deborah Russell

A PAGE UNWRITTEN

    Would truth be oxidated
    and mirrored in the salt?
    though poet, still your words
    echo the concert of distant notes
    flowing in translucent dreams
    you a mirage, a page unwritten
    ink and quill can not still self deception
    would that i could sigh for moon light shadows
    would tranquility glimmer on molecules of air?
    and would enchanting songs of melodic capture
    where movements enrapture me
    imprisoned by your pen?

Debra Marie Reilly

LITTLE GIRL STAR

She struts like a vixen
on every polished stage
within a million mile radius
of childhood

Her mother
(real mother?)
waits in the wings
cross-armed,
iron-fisted,
dollars protruding
through elegant fingers
dipped in red nails

The child
has been modified
into an adult,
tender,
fake breasts
bouncing an unnatural rhythm
to someone else's music

A jeweled navel
highlights her small
naked midrif,
a sparkling oasis
in a teenage wasteland

She expertly swings
unfruitful, narrow hips
designed to mesmerize
young virgin hopefuls
and tired men
old enough to be her father
but grateful they aren't

She groans
more than sings
in a eunuchs voice,
because
that's supposed to be sexy
on a little girl

After the show,
she retreats
to a gilded hotel suite
crawls
into her king-size throne
reaches
under the bed
and retrieves a beat-up shoebox
from her old,
normal room
and regular life

And lifting the lid
she scoops out
her Barbie twin
then
goes into a trance
as she comb's the doll's
phony cornsilk hair

She soothes herself
by rocking
then begins,
in her little girl voice
"hush little baby, don't say a word"
and she doesn't.

Del Senkbeil

A SLAVE TO LOVE

      I feel like a slave
      Put in shackles every day.
      Not free to do what I want to do,
      Or say what I want to say.

      I feel like a lioness
      Pacing around in a cage.
      Trying to find a way out
      Of this difficult, intricate maze.

      Someone's tugging on my heart strings,
      Everytime I'm alone with him.
      My poor heart is trying to tell me,
      This is just a crazy whim.

      Maybe it is, dear heart of mine,
      But I adore him, can't you see?
      So whatever happens in the future,
      I'll have this beautiful memory.

Dianne M. Sherwin

UNSENT LETTERS

I write you letters every day,
letters I don't send

Hoping that each letter helps
this aching heart to mend

I write and tell you of my love
and how it might have been

The laughing, loving, caring...
life worthwhile again

I tell you of my love so true
and what you mean to me

Of dreams and of all other things,
I'd hoped we'd always be

But those letters, never sent,
are only for my eyes

With so many questions
and with no replies

Warm teardrops falling as I write,
upon this letter of love

another unsent message,
that you won't know of....

Dustin

PALE HORSE

Hidden within each of us is demise
residing in our fear.

Like a leech draining our lies
bowing without care.

It creeps to the clepsydra for highs
howling to the pale mare.

A deep Hydra in disguise
sawing into time so dear.

Sans breath it cuts the ties
knowing that our time is near.

At last death fills our eyes
ripping us in a final tear.

Ed Zipek

LATIN LOVER

    Latin lover, olive bronzed
    and smooth to the touch
    ravenous hair always moist
    and lips stilled in
    an array of poses always
    unlocking my soul

    latin boy, black and blue
    let me dress your wounds
    while i remove
    your white calvin's
    over soft callused feet

    latin friend, let me taste
    salty droplets glazing
    glowing cheeks————satisfaction

    latin man, cherished forever
    and before
    missed on
    lonely
    noches de sabado
    when removing makeup—
    just enough to cover your absence.

Edith A. Jenkins

CHORD

A chord is a consequence. It accosts
as if called for, as if called up,
incorporating all that has gone before.
The long apologetic arpeggio of years
hankers behind it
so that we organize memory,
record, disquiet, censor,
and our censorious selves lift
a curtain of the revealed
only to shut it down, a drama
where the actors fail, cough, exempt
themselves with forgetfulness.

I traverse memory with a large eraser
so that islands of events move
into glamorous certitude or fade into reverie,
shout their irreverence and terror,
bleed into pallor.

Chord, recording yourself, all that remains,
all that is past, all that is present.
Record, Oh record.

Elisha Porat

PAINFUL BIRDS

The helicopters, skillful, painful birds,
Again bombard targets above my head:
I sit, shaking at my writing desk,
I bend down to my notebook, clench
My shuddering pen. As if they know...
As if they sense an inner tracer, a red laser
Signal: they make another bomb run,
This time circling above my aging heart,
Who hastens to remove its rooms and
And empty spaces as though they had become
Black tanks, easy targets, sluggish vehicles
Flooded by grief and suffering.

(Translated from the Hebrew by the author and Ward Kelley)

Elsy Satheesan

CHURNING OUT BEATITUDE

A few tricks up your sleeve
And you churn out sheer beatitude!
Out of this marshy life!

Beware, one foot is in the swamp already.
Fix the other on Terra Firma
As best as you can.

Take the stem of robust labor
With petals of love, care, concern
Sincerity and charity.

Churn right and left
Left and right
As fast as you can and as long.

See what emerges!
The pure elixir of simple beatitude!
Want to try it together with me?

Emma Burgin

ASBSENCE

There is an absence of color in my life.
It's a whirlwind of white and gray.
I walk down the street every morning,
Feeling the hard pavement beneath my feet.
When I reach my destination,
I see a glimpse of color:
A small spec of blue in
A pair of beautiful eyes.

Elvira Selow

DADDY'S DIME

once a week she did
cashing-up. noted costs of
soap, pencils, potatoes
(no movies, no books),
piled figures on small pieces
of paper, then with the tone
of a customs inspector
demanded to see the contents
of daddy's pocket - "you must have
two dollars and forty-one cents" -

her voice contained more
ammonia when he had gone
downtown before to buy jerry cottons.
one day he did not return - a streetcar
had dragged him a hundred yards -
she cooked semolina with lumps
and tears, said now he can't read
that trash any more, why didn't he
stay at home

he obeyed but after the counting
used to pull out a coin or two with a
smuggler's grin and rejoice "ha!
a dime"
es

Eve Hall

I PRAY NOT

Is this my destiny...
Never to fall in love
Never to be united as one
Never to share sensual pleasures
Never to come home to someone waiting.

Is this my destiny...
Always having candlelit dinners alone
Always wearing perfumes for no one to smell
Always feeling sexy with no one touching
Always wanting to hear those three little words?

Is this my destiny...
Forever being used and abused
Forever being misunderstood
Forever crying myself to sleep
Forever being unloved?

F. William Broome

A SINGLE ORANGE

Rarest of fruits its golden skin
readily peeled and sectioned
the rare treat of fresh tartness
found only in a single orange.

Finding immeasurable pleasure
as a small child at Christmas
in small gifts a book a toy a few nuts
two apples but only a single orange.

Coveted by all for exquisite taste
its pungent aroma and singular flavor
filling a universal craving to taste
the juicy pulp of a single orange.

Its curative powers benefiting
young and old with illnesses
needing a ready source of Vitamin C
basic nutrition found in a single orange.

Unobtainable during World War II days
occupying an entire jeweler's window
admired and desired by Londoners,
none other but a single orange.

A tasteful wonder of exquisite joy
awarded to anyone discovering

the collective secret
released from a single orange.

A SWING AT SUNSET

In the cool autumn evening
it sits unused
moving slightly in the wind
offering quiet relaxation
as life nears perfection
we choose to sit in our front porch swing.

It begins as a whim
do it before winter
and catch the sun ending its day
while noting that we're on time
for a colorful show
under a canopy of orange and blue.

A glorious orange ball is the star
its sky and clouds perform on cue
as it all comes together
in an array of design
as we watch silently
for fear it might hear us and fade.

Minutes of swinging now and then
gasping in acceptance
shaking heads at the wonder of it all
pointing to places
not to be missed
before it changes into fading tints.

Together we watch
we sigh we bathe ourselves

in the wash of gorgeous hues
bursting with quiet joy
and knowing the other is feeling
deep unspoken content.

Filipe Miguel Gomes

AS I FOUND YOU

And suddenly
something I felt
stood quiet
confused . . . .
in my heart a fast beat.
Was it fear, fantasy?
And more it was,
was happiness, emotion,
willingness to scream
loud, very loud
my love, oh, my love
everything for me you are
everything for you I will be.
. . .and calm
quiet I stood.
Felt weak, lost in thoughts.
I know now I have you
you are mine, my love
you are life, soul and dream
you are night, you are desire
. . .on you I lay down,
on you I rest.
I feel good, in love.
If I have you, I'm everything
if I lose you, nothing I am.

Francis Figueroa

HER PAIN

As I sit helplessly watching her in pain,
It slowly begins to drive me insane.
I wish to take her pain and keep it as mine,
Because then she would be just fine.
Even though I have a great pain of my own,
I know we won't be together it's just me alone.
I just can't stand seeing her hurt like that,
I would die to make her feel better and that's a fact.
It doesn't matter though, in the end, what I want,
Whoever controls my life would rather just taunt.

Frank Anthony

MY NURSE WAS PEDOPHILE

>What good does it ever
>do to wonder about the
>way I had been treated
>by someone in the past
>Father never wanted me
>Mother thought of self
>Brother broke my bones
>Sister of another mark
>Our all American start
>got me off to the race
>no way I can ever quit
>right up to the finish
>the old game is a mess

Addendum

>*Have Your Own Good Day.* In this lucid dream I am getting into the circuits that really make a difference. All the symbols indicate: The way an embryo is affected by mother blood, fondled by a nurse and treated by parents and siblings, is IT. You are either in competition or in love with life. After eight or ten years, one possibly may try to change. However, the systemic nature, of human society, pulls you back into the race for survival, difficult in a competitive atmosphere. If you are fortunate enough, be true to yourself, with luck you may escape the jackals. All there ever is to life.

Fred Marmorstein

CADGER

Mother stands, impossible, the way dignity chases the wild
rushing forward, keeping the seemingly innocent together
begging me to struggle as she has struggled

She wants to celebrate images of dark gowns
and blue mortarboards tasseled blue
strengthened against the slide
of square degree down my face, a piece of cardboard
tight on my head

She appears like a corner
an arid chance fretting
cutting hesitation away
she swells, laughs from the stage, beggar of a different breed
to feed the wonder why I have no time for you

Growing old, she shrouds earthly answers
dampens old melodies
her heart is triple time
punishing the least damaged
protecting what she sees before me.

Gary Lehmann

WALT WHITMAN IN WASHINGTON

After years of comforting Union soldiers in shabby hospitals at his own expense,
Walt Whitman was appointed to a small office in the Bureau of Indian Affairs.
Stylizing himself the "poet chief of the Whitman,
"Whitman received Indian delegations in the basement of the Patent Office,
surrounded by old patent models.
The chiefs appeared silently before him, like dry desert winds in strange costumes.
They came to talk of broken treaties and payments that had mysteriously disappeared.
Whitman listened attentively to their complaints and then explained,
"We are all one." "You are my brothers." "Your joys and sorrows are my very own."
"I feel with you."
The chiefs looked at each other in their feathers and buckskin, and asked, "how?"

WATCHING THE BEACH — 1066 AD

A moment exists just before full dark, known to every sailor,
a bewitching moment hovering between bleak magic and the breath of sanctity,
just after the sun sets and just before darkness envelops the earth
when the wind slackens and the moon creeps over the water like a tiger.
In this pregnant moment, the water winds give way to the land winds.
In just such an awkward moment, neither day nor night, on Hastings Beach,

I waited with anxiety and fear as fine sailing ships, bristling with French soldiers,
came to rest a few hundred yards from my English shore.
All day long I waited, transfixed by this mysterious visitation,
powerless to abate its menace or silence its neighing horses.
Too young to turn this tide, caught in cross currents, neither man nor boy,
I stood watching on, too proud to hide, too small to fight, too curious to run away.
Like me, the winds had too many ways to turn and no where to go.
The father of the wind called me home. My mother called out, "Come to shore."
The French William for his part also waited for the wind to make up its mind.
Anxious soldiers tried rowing, but were silenced with a gesture.
In time, the foundling sun dropped down and the night wind emerged,
as we knew it would, urging the French onward toward blood-lust.
Tiny zephyrs arrived from the land, and then from the sea, and then the land again.
Lines were made taut. I hid in the tall green grass to brace myself for slaughter.

Geraldine Sarmiento

HONESTLY SORRY

I was weak but still you loved the weakness within me
I was hopeless but you showed me there could be tomorrow
I could not fly but you taught me not to crawl
I was scared and you made me feel strong

I was hurting and endlessly crying
you held your hand and showed you care
I was unforgiving full of hatred in my heart
but you told me there is no good in hate
and forgave me so I could learn to forgive

I was to the point of giving up
almost to letting go
but you said hold on, maybe someday, somehow

you told me, "I love you"
but you taught me to much
I cannot let go, I can no longer lie to myself
I know you wish you haven't taught me that much
but please do understand, if you honestly care

listen to what I say, I do mean each word
thank you for all that you've been but I cannot love you still
but until that day do keep in mind that maybe someday, somehow.

Geertruud Ida Maria

UNVEILED FUTURE

Thin valuable veil of perpetual brainwaves
Hide the fairy silk face of a true soul
Mystique eyes, mirrors of present moments
Stare at hazy pictures of future events
Diamond ears, receivable shells of direct sound
Listen to silent noises framed by tomorrow
Nostrils inhale air spread by the invisible now
Smell sensual fragrances evaporated soon
Ruby soft lips touch volatile feelings
Taste indefinite forthcoming flavors

The here and now soaked by all past
Embodies all present impressions
Senses transparent treasures in the offing
Through a natural curtain that covers
A beautiful face into coming existence
By clear insight of a mindless soul
Like the soft thin veil of a future bride
Removed by the impatient groom
Looking for tomorrows dowry.

BURNING QUESTIONS

Wrapped up in slow nocturnal light
Hundreds of small flickering flames
Circle around me in the middle of the night
Kindled by dear ones with no names

The fresh flower fragrance so fair
Dispel thousand tedious thoughts now
Burned by my fires right into the air
All questions, like why when and how

Disarming smiles the lights seem to be
The ones you can see in a little baby face
Soothing presents heaven sends to me
Touched by guardian angels full of grace
Curled up I dream, a dream of delight
While the candles go out one by one
The day will overtake this holy night
Awakening my soul by her bright sun.

Ginny Christiansen

FRACTURED FAIRYTALE

You rode in upon your mighty steed
To rescue this damsel in her hour of need
We galloped through fields of fragrant flowers
Then we'd make love and talk for hours
My hair was flowing as we trotted the shore
Then we'd make love and make love some more
I thought the sun rose and set in your eyes
And heaven was found in your contented sighs
I thought happily ever after was how fairytales went
But my heart finally got messages that my head sent
What I thought was your love, was nothing but lust
When I looked at your armor, it was pockmarked with rust
You not a knight, your steed a tired old nag
I not a princess, just a lonely old hag
Once upon a time, was how it began
But now is the end of the story and that toad of a man....

Giovanni Ghirga MD

I WOULD LIKE TO BE MAD

I would like to be mad
Not to understand the truth

To dream by day
And not to think looking

Not to hear screaming
And not to see the suffering

Not to love myself
And no to fear death

Like Saint Francesco
I would like to be mad
To rid myself
Of my belonging

Because I am desperate
Since I understood.

Goldie Mae

DESTINY DANCING ACROSS A CHESS BOARD

Black and white marbled figures, dainty and straight
A challenging game dancing with fate,
Our ideas on life our other chess pieces,
While we are the masterminds attempting escape.

I flirt dangerously close to the bordering brink,
Of problems that are seemingly unsolvable,
Just as I think that perhaps the play is at an end,
A brilliant new move is made on our chessboard again.

Much similar to the two tango dancers,
Which seem to move with striking grace,
Like fencing we fight,
You lunge, I parry, my hearts defended.

Time for a new dance where I'm the aggressor,
Seductive feminine whiles used to lure,
While teasing and taunting till you're at breaking point,
I smile knowingly, intellectually, a perfect play.

Still in the same game, the chess match goes on,
Playing each other, making mistakes, we move on,
Until one day it strikes us, we both won in this game,
In love forever, our hearts are lightened from life's dreary chains.

Gregory W Bryant

I WILL BE THERE

When the sub refuses to shine;
and you think you are losing your mind;
I will be there.

If your day is sunny and bright;
and you need to share some of that light;
I will be there.

When your nights are lonely and cold;
and you need someone to caress and to hold;
I will be there.

All I'm trying to say and express;
if you are feeling sad, happy or stressed;
I will be there.

Harold Janzen

I WOULD TRAVEL ALL THE LIGHT YEARS

I would travel all the light years
from the beginning till now
just to touch the first heart
traveling within the mind's resistance
to go that far

I would travel to the end
of the next line singing
forever thru the endless
mirage I'd walk
to reach start

listen
I would travel
in a circle
to rewind the matter of every part
I'd unravel the mystery

I would travel all the light years
from the beginning
of things.

Heather La Croix

UNION

Patience my enemy,
Pride my whore
Waxing, waning, wanting, waiting
Eternally shining the impetuous cycle
Of my light
On your silken shore
We, both of us, ebb tho
And sometimes the light hits just right
And it is beautiful...

Heather Johnson

MICHAEL THE ANGEL

>Michael the angel.
>Michael the fool.
>Micheal the smart one.
>Michael schooled.
>
>Michael who loved me,
>his best talent.
>Michael who left me,
>what was his intent?
>
>Michael was everything
>I'd ever want.
>Michael's love
>will forever haunt.
>
>Michael my lover.
>Michael my friend.
>Michael who left me.
>Why did it have to end?

I'll never forget him. He won't become passe.
I'll live alone, forever, in memories of those days.
Days of love songs. Written words from the heart.
Days I believed in him and knew we'd never part.
His words are etched deep in my memory.
I still close my eyes and feel him holding me.

H. G. Brown

THE LISTENING ROOM

A friend of mine designed a listening room,
A place where foliage and music bloom
In concert: wandering jew and succulent;
Mozart, Miles, and spider plant.

He offers tea, I accept.
Before he turns to where the kettle's kept
He lowers stylus into groove to play
A String quartet recalled from yesterday.

I think the world was quiet then, more still
The time that one endured, the nights more still.

Now, even potted palms might rejoice
To hear this counterpoint, these lambent chords.
The infinitely baffled speakers voice
A heart-to-heart that leaves me wanting words.

Hiram Larew

ACCIDENT

There are two types of people in the world
Ones who care about tires
And ones who wear color
Both like to drive
And both get lost
Especially when they are looking for
Each other

There are also two kinds of roads around here
Some that plow straight ahead
And others on vacation
Where they meet is tricky
Because it always seems to be somewhere else
Not here

Look there are even two kinds of soup waiting
Some with fish and carrots
And others free as spring
Eventually one becomes as awful as the other
But not before both get given away
Like steam on mirrors
Proudly shyly.

Howard Camner

OFFSPRING RHAPSODY

I breathe carefully now
I watch where I walk and when
She's learned how her hands work
She's learned how I work
She drops things knowing I'll pick them up
She's learned to laugh
She's learned to cry
(and so have I)
Her temper is mine
Her serenity; her mother's
I'm more afraid of people now
because I know what you're capable of
(and what you're not capable of)
I know all the train songs
and the wisdom of Seuss
I check the locks a thousand times
to keep you out
(to keep you in)
I inhale for wolves
I inhale for thieves
and I watch her when she sleeps
wondering what she dreams.

Isadora SuZhen Snapp

YOU HAVE TRIED

You have tried your hardest
to break us down,
to fill our hearts with fear,
but still, we will pick up the pieces
and overcome you all.

You have separated us from our families
and burnt our wisest amongst your flames of hate,
but still, we shall come together
and believe again in our faith.

You have tried your hardest
to make us cry,
but those tears you see are ones of pride
for within our souls we hide the secret
of life and immortality.

And although you have
spilled our blood,
we are still millions strong,
and from the ashes of our pain,
again and again,
we will rise above you all.

Jack Conway

AND ALLEN GINSBERG IS MOPPING UP IN AISLE NINE

I been waxing poetic over you,
when I should have been waxing the floor —
Not no more, baby — Not no more.
Got no more time for rhymes,
(but I got some in mind).

Don t want no bee in my bonnet over no sonnet —
I got aisles to go before I sweep
and you know they love to watch me lap the aisles.

Swear I m gonna change, baby —
Ain t gonna be chasing you around for no sextain —
I got enough words for us —
Got me a rhyming dictionary and a brand new thesaurus.

Hey, I know I could use a good lai,
but I can t stop,
I got to mop this place —
Ain t nobody gonna save my assets
if it ain t done —
Aye, that s the scrub.

What we got here is a pile of broken glass and foam
no time for poems —

And what I need, baby, what I need is an annuity,
not ambiguity.

I know, I know, baby —
Ambiguity celebrates the pleasures of doubt,
but not outta my mouth.

I can t sustain no quatrain,
no meter,
no rhyme —
Ain t got no time — No time.
You want to see poetry in motion, baby — ?
I'll show you poetry in motion —
Just give me some room and hand me a broom.

There s poetry enough all over this place —
poets in the produce,
rhymes in the check-out line,
sonnets in the soda,
lyrics in the syrup,
ballads in the bakery,
fresh couplets hanging in the deli —
(Now, there s a bunch of boloney —)
And someone s always bagging the free verse.

I know the story — memento mori —
You think I don t know that baby— ?
You think I don t know—?

Look at me —
What you see — ?
Some pentameter janitor —?
Not no more, baby — Not no more.

The only verse worth anything is up your skirt, baby
and you know my pen is ready.

J. D. Nelson

LOADED W/ CREATURES

On the road
with a Roman rose
in my chimp teeth:

a parking lot symphony
of dogs & babies
left to broil
in unmarked cars

beady
little
eyes
glowing.

Jan Oskar Hansen

THE OPERA SINGER

They found him in a field
of poppies, weed and
flowering almond trees.
Slowly sinking into ground,
the skin on his face had
the colour of soil.
A nuisance when alive
singing rude songs keeping
us awake at night.
Now he lies on a spot
where an evergreen bush
shall shimmer in the sun.
...And his soul will smile
when seeing us hastening by,
on the road to nowhere.

A ROMANCE REMEMBERED

Morning sadness by the kitchen
table remembering a woman
I once loved...Do I still? Or is it
the memory of my infatuation that
I love? Can't see her face clearly
anymore, but sense her embraces,
sweet breath and soft voice, after
love, something about:" Forever"

On returning from the sea she had
married and moved away. Spring
darkened, a chilly wind blew my
youth into cynical middle age.
I should have called on her if only
to finalize the ending, as it is
the unspoken is a barrier to what
could have been a sweet memory.
Now that I shall not see her again,
too many years have dripped and
made tiny holes on the sandstone
of time, only the faint echo of her
whispering voice remains:
"Forever, forever my love."

THE SHRIEK

The bar's door opened and a nicotine infested
shaft of light was thrown out. Above corny
music, hoarse laughter. The door slammed
shut and the hurt but not mortally so, shaft
crawled along the kerb climbed a lamppost
and blended with dejected yellow light.
Underneath the lamppost, a badly lit stage,
a woman, scantly dressed, stood she had
something to sell, but in the dismal light
her face looked like a death mask and since
there were few necrophiliacs about, on this
slow Monday night, she had to wait long
before she could go back into the bar and
seek comfort amongst fellow losers.
On the other side of the street a bus stopped,
wheezing doors opened, for a moment she
had an audience of stony faced shift workers

going home, they didn't applaud her heroic
effort to look sexy. Diesel fume wafted through
still air and come to rest on murky asphalt as
a sullied rainbow.
When the bus left her body shrunk, tears found
cracks in a ruined face and the echo of a silent
scream shifted dust on pavements.

THE TRAIL

It's an old trail, old as the landscape; older than
the trees, which exposed roots boldly cross it like
petrified brown snakes. Mule hooves and man
have made it deep and barren, but now that few
walk to the hamlet it leads to; green shoots are
coming up through cracks in hard soil. No one
lives in the hamlet anymore haven't done so for
years, now reduced to a pile of stones, a memorial
to the passing of time and the ultimate futility of
human toil. Through and behind the hamlet the trail
continues, fainter now almost invisible like a fine scar
across a beautiful face making it hauntingly mysterious.
The trail abruptly ends at the foot of an ancient oak and
beyond, that marker, the hot breath of a bush landscape,
that rolls up a hill till it merges with low clouds and disappears
into a haze of nothingness, into a great void where
all humanity will vanish and their tombstone shall be
heap of rocks, which in time will be yellow sand, seashore
on a tropical island.

Jason Clapham

KENTISH OAKS

    Rising out of the lush floodplains
    bark strangely phosphorescent
    in the muddy light of evening
    these oaks are like giant resin casts
    of the vascular system of the brain

    immensely fragile, inconceivably intricate
    a glimpse into that obscure network
    soon to be clothed in a skull of blossom

    they stand waiting patiently
    keeping watch
    self-assured
    for a sun they can faintly recollect.

Jason E. Windham

THE CRAWLING FLESH

    All my veins
    gone black and snaking.
    All that's left,
    this web I'm shaking.
    How am I
    this thing discarded?
    I curse the place where all this started.
    I was sick, his prey,
    and falling.
    He puked thick,
    this flesh now crawling.
    A way to feel has never left me,
    I hate this Earth that failed to bless me.

Jason McIntosh

LONELINESS...

>Another year looms heavily,
>new faces, new people, new lives,
>I sit and look and wonder anew,
>thinking of past encounters,
>and those yet to come,
>so much that is me,
>so much that is you.
>What are we anymore,
>grains of sand in oceans,
>rubbing awhile against each other,
>and fading away into night,
>Do we lose or do we gain,
>new loves, old fears,
>above all a few more tears,
>hearts get broken and things end,
>only as we watch to begin again.
>Why this mad dash, this run,
>why the fear and being alone,
>why do we go on and start again,
>the continual struggle for answers,
>a sea of questioning thoughts.
>We each search and look,
>and we all dream of brighter days,
>for though we know not,
>we hope and look for what is,
>that our purpose may be found,
>and our lives fulfilled.

Jessica Hatton

BLACK TUESDAY

Terror strikes
duty calls
to save the lives
before the tower falls

The clock is ticking
with no time to think
but only to react quickly
without a wink

People panic
people scream
they fear their worst
beyond any dream

They run with fear
and cry with shock
they all go running
in one giant flock

Over the bridges
through the streets
they ran in all directions
by the quickness of their feet

Their voices cried out
for help was heard

look here they come
all in a herd

The sirens rang loud
like one chilling scream
everyone knew...
what this would mean

They heard people's cries
many loud and clear
they have come to rescue us
without any fear

They are the heroes we know
they all ran inside
into a burning building
with no place to hide

It was the day of darkness
a day full of fear
for no one knew
what was near

The towers were to come crashing
in a blink of an eye
with thousands upon thousands
trapped inside

A nightmare, reality
shocking but true
for this was something
no one knew

Screams were heard
tears were shed
who knows where this
will head

The unthinkable has happened
the twins fell
and those who did this
will go to hell

Here we stand
we must unite
we all must come together
and work through the night

Those who are alive
are who we must find
we must begin our search
with no waste of time

Days will become nights
as a night will become a day
those who decided to do this
will soon begin to pay

Our brothers and sisters have died
and you are what's to blame
for this is where hatred has brought us
and ignorance should all be ashamed

Many mourn
many cry
for they did not know
their loved ones would die

Now we remember those who have fallen
and most of all those who ran in to the trouble
they are the heroes we know..
the heroes that lie beneath the rubble

A tragedy, it takes
to open our eyes
it took a whole nation
by surprise

For NOW we must stand
and unite
for we should all by willing
to go and fight

They took our loved ones
and with no shame
but now its our turn
to play their GAME......

Jessie O'Donovan

WOULD YOU?

If I died tomorrow
you'd be in my heart,
but would I be in
yours in some small part?

Would you be sad
and grieve for me,
or would you carry
on and let life be?

Would you remember
me forever on,
or would you forget me
to let our memories be gone?

If to me you could
profess your love,
one last time before
I'm sent above.

Life is too short
to let it roll by,
we should live life to
the fullest before we die.

Jill Chan

COMING HOME

holding an umbrella
sheltering us
from the weeping sky
my father said to me
is that boy courting you?

And this was a guy
who's a friend
he had just given me
a lift on his way home

it was pouring
the rain was answering.

Joan Hambidge

SOLITAIRE

My family, compulsive bridge players,
could easily shuffle
an entire holiday away
with a game of cards.
My father especially, a daunting player,
could teach his children
every trick of the trade.
But with me it was different.
From early on I was cut off
from their hard calls,
their delight over a good hand
or bluff
while they were sitting together at a table
in a holiday town at the sea.
I already listened as a child
silently to the sea's rhythm
and placed imaginary cards
one by one on the roulette wheel.

ONE NIGHT STAND

One night stand
The scene is always the same:
intro-drink-seduction-bed.
The next day constantly a mind fuck:
guilt-silence-longing
and regret.
To fall in love is like placing a bet.

John A Duffy

READY TO GO

I ain't frightened anymore
Found a key through
the door
One step two steps
on the floor
I'm not frightened.
Made my peace said
my prayer
I'm quite sure
you are all aware
That! Just!
Just through there
just beyond the threshold
of the door.
I won't be frightened
anymore.

John Birkbeck

MIGRATORY SPECIES

>I'm parking
>the blue limo
>on the rooftop ramp
>but I'm going down below
>where the action is
>and life is low
>and the lowlifes
>are getting high.
>The girls are faking
>blonde hair again
>from Palm beach to Pompano
>but what the hell!
>If you got it
>you might as well
>fake it . . .no?

EX-EAGLE SCOUT

>Subjective quasi-anarchic
>embryo ideas interject
>stray dreams into literary
>war-stories and maybe two
>language stunts, etc., and
>get a fluffing, a spasmodine.
>The last flushings-out of

madhouses and slammers and
missions and workfarms, eh?
the self-talkings-to and
reasonless leers at passers-by
should (must!) be on a ward
someplace... Instead of where?
Here?

John Dempsey

A NOTE ON 5 AM

    green
    passing soft
    I was
    watching the clouds
    slowly
    eating
    the
    sunshine
    breakfast special

ENTANGLED HOURS...

    There's a sticky, sweet reek
    underneath
    her laughter-

    it's that Kodak smell
    of
    years
    long
    gone-

    and all she has to do is laugh
    for the moments
    to spring back to life.

John Michael Martinez

HOLLOW CONCEPTS

Fragments of before and whats to come,
Making minds numb,
Worldly gimmicks and concepts false,
Duped by half-truths and politics' faults,
Secrets locked in vaults,
Behind closed doors,
Answers are there,
Questions arise even more,
Religious practices,
Against each other's grain,
All this is tiresome,
Let's pretend complacency,
It's fun to be insane,
Love and sincerity,
Is being ignored,
Do people want to be together?
Or are we fighting other peoples wars?

John Western

A SECRET KISS IN A DARK ROOM

I still and will forever, taste your lips
from a secret kiss in a dark room.

As always will remain, the smell of your perfume
that clings to my shirt.

Torment myself do I, while looking at you
through my eyes of wanting and anticipation.

And race, uncontrolled does this heart
of shattered pieces, I hold in my weeping sky.

Down they fall, along with a million tears
cried by the same minds of broken souls.

I question myself, could this friend - to whom I
would present eternity itself, be more than a friend?

But the scent of your melodic essence, that dances
on my collar, doesn't want to let go.

As I still and will forever, taste your lips
from a secret kiss in a dark room.

Joseph Aprile

THERE IS A CERTAIN CATACLYSMIC BEAUTY IN EVERY MOMENT

There is a certain cataclysmic beauty in every moment,
a certain dream-like way we have of propelling ourselves about.

Two heavy glass doors of the bank each bearing the word push,
a priest and his ministry watching
as the local parishioners steal the polish off the rectory furniture,
a patrol car turns a corner at sunset,
two old men in the park accost each other with chess pieces,
one lonely candle burns in the temple,
on the desert a gun is raised and yet another viewpoint is
extinguished.

A man and his lady
their shadows jerk and spin,
an empty bottle of gin,
factory smoke,
in Harlem glass is pushed out of windows
in preparation for summer,
a sprawling restless suburb spews out its traffic towards megalopolis.

Space and stars and the cosmic wind eyed by poets
and admirers of faraway things.

Rushing wind of tree light amber carries wild ponies along the crests
of fiery dreams,
capricious captains of wayward sails and blind wood bearers worship
visions of god and the chaos he engenders,

the seasons mark the weathering of earth in time's embrace as Homo
Sapiens tentatively walks its surface.

Light transfigures the islands of the sun
in the voluptuous ring of fire where
Vulcan maintains his kingdom,
the earth sails round and round in its arc of heaven where the Greeks
once nimbly held the rudder,
sail on sail on proud earth though your rulers be forsaken.

Two guitarists at the window by the night,
the moon glides gingerly over the sounds of humanity,
the air is filled and we awaken to it like gypsies,
blood and violence both rushing over sanguine dreams,
the hypnotist and his magician hand in hand in the alley,
the highway motions, the sea distorts,
and the heart empties its vessels.

Brick upon brick,
the worn patterns of the ancients,
the brooding whispers of the virgins of the clotheslines,
Sunday morning newspapers,
and the hock shops.
Moon glides into the vault of the sky,
frog cadence push up into the still air
beneath the cloth of darkness,
oblique shadows briefly interrupt the moment,
life stands like a calamity above the birth of spring,
a lonely scotch broom catches the air by the side of the highway,
two billboards disguised by nightfall wait until dawn
to capture the eyes of motorists who have
forgotten the majesty of trees.

Words are caught and vaulted into the morning air,
the sounds they impart to the wind land on nothing in particular,

solitary bodies move in jaunty strides to park benches
where bottles of wine leap out of hip pockets
into fish-like mouths and ultimately
into brandied circulation to deliver
a vital numbness to perception,
shrinking time into a
singular cup of liquid tension,
cavalier gentlemen with their lives' work packed on their backs,
stake out their concrete niches,
men of past and future miseries
dream of other worlds to take comfort in.

The ebb and flow of foliage under time's capitulation
comforts the earthbound with its familiarity,
the short gray tedious light of winter with its long damp nights
and the rain streaking across wet windows,
the obscure moon and creeping inevitable cold
as it lurches along the ground and
permeates the seasoned wood of the house,
and swells itself into the bones and the space of the room.

The idle hermit-like croaking of a frog
who forgot his hibernating ways,
the deer who descend from secret habitations to taste
the fallen red fruit beneath the apple trees
always with ears funneled to catch the faintest sounds,
the rain, the infernal rain,
tempering the everything with its relentless rhythm
degrading and demolishing everything.

Sad, sad William moves along the black monument
bathed in the unsettling mist of midnight air,
he moves along its polished surface with a trembling hand,
searching for the names of his dead comrades,
the great capitol looms nearby but offers no solace,

on finding the chiseled memory of his friends,
on feeling the recognition come at last,
sad, sad William wings his heart skyward,
in unabashed joy!
relief at last to a burdened spirit,
his tears sing of a lost generation.

Life is a chain of light and dark,
brain shapes meaning from escapades of form and shadow,
without night there is no detail,
no delineation of beginning from its end,
no respite from the merciless truth.

The morning stretches across the household trash,
and an old crumpled newspaper on the porch,
it is winter and the snow being not quite so unfamiliar
falls with both rapture and cunning,
the dew on sleeping eyes,
the spider
its fly in web near stone,
there is a plane in the sky overhead,
and the thoughts from it descend
on a forest of robust illusions,
on a lonely mountain in California,
astronomers from the college are
trying to capture the sun in a mirror.
Ice is melting in the river,
time is polishing the rocks and slowly they diminish themselves
so that the wind might release them from the burdens of gravity,
sand releases the desert of its heat,
the stark white ice of mountains,
the towering ice that spirals beneath the breath of intellects,
the cold hunger of nations chasing the empires
billowing in their heads,
the dance of heat and ice beneath the moon's escape.

The lady is naked now, and caresses her body
with stiff white hands,
her toes rub against the night,
her lips stretch across the open sky,
no one to receive them,
the lady has no ears to hear
the loves that have eluded her,
the walls of the apartment speak of nothing
except their own morbid perfection,
the lady sits by her tenacity and
forever misses the caravan outside of her window,
she knows no one else's story and seldom dreams,
the lady is naked now and weeps
between the crevices of her curtains,
she will be mourned at the cinema,
the clock on the dresser has a cracked face,
the hair brush is pearl-handled and meticulous,
there is no mirror,
one photograph of mother and a box of kleenex,
the air barely stirs inside.

The street cleaner,
his cracked lips and parchment features,
his cigarette dangling among the smoke of private thoughts,
the bus stop,
the gas station,
the doors of stores and restaurants are opened,
morning coffee waits patiently in kitchens
for men stumbling out of their werewolf dreams,
the women and their silent bravado.
The town lies in its contradictions,
a candle and mirror to a bewildering age,
nearby, the mountains cradle their momentous glaciers
silently catching stray planes,
whose pilots failed to measure the proper attitude of retreat.

Humans with their thinking and planning
remain solemnly in their shelters,
as the wind marks its way across the prairie,
the cows and cattle graze,
the sun finds its way to a hillside
where it plummets and ignites the watchful clouds
to a final charcoal finish.

The world is a place of cycles and unfinished remembrances,
churches are built and once a year
the Messiah climbs back on his cross,
and once a year the pilgrims seek their admonitions,
droughts come and go,
calves fall like timber in heavy spring blizzards,
the Romans came and left highways,
and a certain yearning for architecture,
flowers and flies and tumbleweeds
all have their seasons.

Bells in their stolid churches,
old people walking upright
like the old reeds they are
keep memories of their children
in the air above them as they move about,
and gather themselves at noon on benches
where they exchange both rude and pleasant things.

Children are too much like their parents,
and parents so much like their kin,
that there are always petty crimes and jealousies,
and to every family there are born upstarts,
who hold up mirrors, mockingly,
but, there is always laughter.

Old kingdoms fall stubbornly,
and death is usually premature,
delight and tragedy mingle at the borders,
but, there is always laughter.

Humans carry the ghosts of many tongues,
and the dormant remembrances
of the great forest and endless seas.

The woman pushes our her first born at forest's edge,
a young fox looks on with a kind of recognition
of the majesty of the event,
she caresses her baby and reignites the essence of her race,
the engine of life continues.

There is a certain cataclysmic beauty in every moment,
a certain dream-like way we have of propelling ourselves about.

Karen Alkalay-Gut

STAINS

People with long
Memories for pain
Scare me no end
Especially
When it is the pain
Of insult the reminder

Each year
Deepening the scar
The creases the fissure
The wound.

Kari Marie Gilbert

RAINSTORM

    Thunder rolling
    raindrops
    pitter-patter on the roof
    hold me
    close tight safe warm
    in your strong arms
    thunder
    crash
    crack
    don't let go
    hold me love.

Kathie Isaac-Luke

KINETICS

You know what they say about a rolling stone—
that nothing clings to it.
As though the acquisition of moss were a virtue.
As though it were better to rest encumbered
than skip solitary down the face of a hill.

We make our choices.
There are storage spaces for what we cannot carry.
And everything that I have wanted to hold near
proved as ephemeral as smoke—
or as a sigh.

Kathleen K. Harris

THE MELODY OF RENEWAL

Poetry is the unfurling of wings.
Sing to me of Spring's approach
Of gossamer wing and rainbow coach
To peek an eye from Winter's sleep
Of whistling winds and raindrops weep

Sing to me as seasons change
From woolen rags to pastel range
Dressed elegant in formal fines
Of blossoms fair and silken twines

Sing to me of Spring's new morn
Of new returns as hope is born
To dawn another day so sweet
Of weather warm in kind repeat.

Kathleen Lawlor

BEHIND CLOSED DOORS

Do you ever wonder
what goes on behind closed doors?
So many possibilities;
so many situations.
Is there someone there
filled with anger?
Is there someone there
filled with love?
It will always be a mystery;
what goes on behind closed doors.
What you see
isn't always what is real.
Behind closed doors
the fascades are shed.
It's scary sometimes
to look behind those doors.
Do you ever wonder
what goes on behind closed doors?

Kathleen Rose Cruger

BLUEBIRD STORM

What happened to justice?
The hate has bloomed like a flower after a
Storm.
I don't understand.
How can something as mystical as a blossom,
Be related to that storm.
Jealousy.
A monster locked within.
His cage only opened by the happiness of
Another.
The eyes cry out of envy and rage.
The happy should littered with salty tears
Of violence.
Perception altered.
From life to death;
From spring to winter;
Light to darkness.
The monster rages on like a blizzard in May.
Confusing.
The sacred heart unjustly bound.
Tired.
Longing for the bluebird of spring to once
Again grace this tormented land.
But the winter storm swallowed the bluebird.
The monster has won.
Envy and rage captured the innocent heart.
The storm wiped out the
Last
Lowly
Blossom.

Kazuyosi Ikeda

SUMMER AND WINTER

The floating clouds in summer seem to be burning.
Tormented by the sunlight dazzling and severe,
The blades of grass gasp for breath, with great suffering.
They wait the coming autumn, cool, bracing and clear.

Lo, white and deep blue compose a fine striped pattern.
The midsummer's sea assumes a deep blue colour.
The foaming waves, forming stripes, are white like silver.
Nature makes a beauteous, exquisite pattern.

A mosquito is buzzing; his voice is so thin
That the sadness increases on a summer's night.
Once approaching me, he bites my delicate skin;
The itch conveys to my heart his grief of tonight.

In winter the snow, lying deep on the mountains,
In phantom cotton bedding for mountain grasses.
All grasses sleeping in snow die on the mountains,
Before mild spring comes again: piteous grasses!

Over the fields I wonder alone in winter.
By chance I find a holly blooming stealthily.
Its petals are virgin-white, charming and lovely.
Like the smell of my love's skin is its sweet odour.

O my sweetheart! I will hold thy hands in my hands.
Virgin-white snow has fallen and lies on the road.
Throw off thy deeply red gloves on the snow-white road
So that I can hold thy hands warmly in my hands.

Kenneth McManus

SAMBA SINGER

Stretched out lazily
Across South Pacific breezes
Gauguin sketches playing across the mind
Ripe mangoes coming into season,
Gentle summonses from Nature
To find one rhythm
Persimmon brown, pink seeds bursting forth
From suave bossa nova waves
Catching the hesitancy
'Twixt the transition from
Modern to natural
Played out in varying tempos
As we wait for next tango,
Next bolero, next bird call
Proxima languid leap
Across a sleepy chasm
Of vocal charm.

Kevin James Knowles

BALLAD OF A FIREFIGHTER ON SEPTEMBER 11TH

He donned his red jacket
and laced up his boots.
Too bad for him fighting fires
was in his family roots.

"Bye, honey!" he yelled as
he walked towards the door.
He thought today would be
like every other before.

"Don't worry about me.
I'll be all right."
It's just another day,
I'll see you tonight."

How was anybody to know
that four birds guided by hate
would devastate a nation
and engrave such a date.

When the first plane struck
it took our nation by surprise.
The crowds were in disbelief.
You could see it in their eyes.

The second plane impacted
the side of Tower Two.
People watched in horror.
There was nothing they could do.

"No, this can't be!" she cried
as she watched it unfold.
"He said not to worry.
He'll be fine, I was told."

Firefighters rushed to the scene
and ran in brave as could be,
never thinking of their own lives,
just wanting to get people free.

And free them they did.
They saved many lives,
But this is the real world
and not everyone survives.

Kevin M. Horsley

SAD EYE'S

My sad eye's are cryin' for you darling,
you've chosen to leave me alone.
I cannot sleep at night,
and I don't think I can go on.

There's a big empty spot,
in my bed as well as my heart.
My empty heart cries,
ever since we fell apart.

My sad eye's watch for you out the window,
every Saturday.
Cause' that's the day you'd come to me,
and my heart would get carried away.

I look back on our memories together,
my sad eye's cry once more.
I just want things to be back,
to the way they were before.

Kimberly Beth Nelson

TITLE

My own phoenix sprang from our ashes
rainbow plumage,
mighty wings,
it flew by in hopes of teaching my heart to sing.
it looked into my eyes,
my mind and soul,
showed my the pieces I'd dropped
in hopes of remaking me as a whole.
and so I was forced to relearn Kim,
as seen through my own eyes,
not as viewed by him.

WEDNESDAY MORNING

My brains a mess
my stimachs worse
oh how I love this horrible cuse
Firewater, devils piss
the ecstasy of Satan's kiss
what I look for I cannot find
so I'll numb my soul, my heart, my mind
my genie in a bottle,
a granted wish for every sip
my delusions I coddle,
as I struggle to get a grip.

Kirby Wright

OBSERVATIONS FROM OCEANSIDE, CALIFORNIA

The beach is nearly deserted.
Sandpipers scuttle,
then stab the wet sand
with beaks.
A jogger appears
then disappears
into a mirage
rising off the strand.
The day smells industrial.
A power plant to the south
sends black plumes
out of its tower.
A man paddles a boogie board
through the shallows.
Offshore, a gray destroyer
treads water. It seems
as harmless as
a bathtub toy.
The war is a distant thing
where men, women
and children die
beyond the bent horizon.

Kristine

MY K9 ANGEL

I believe in angels and
now I truly know,
that you were sent from up above
and how I love you so.

It all began eight years ago,
on a day I'll never forget
K9 angel it was a wonderful moment,
the instant our eyes met.

You may not wear a halo or have
wings for you to fly,
but you have a heart so full of love
and such caring big brown eyes.

K9 angel you're always near, no
matter what may be
and even on a most difficult day, you're
there to comfort me.

You have enriched my life so much
more than words can say,
Thank you, my best friend for the
joy you bring each day.

Yes I believe in angels cause
one watches over me, day and
night he gives me love,
friendship and loyalty.

Kristina Anna Lehner

TEENIE LIFE

No one seems to
understand you,
you stand alone
against the whole world,
noone listens,
noone cares,

That is
what all of us
sometimes feel,
and sometimes
it is true.

Why should we mind
what happens to you,
what you think
or what you feel?
We have lives
of our own,
so what interest
would we take in yours?

That is
what many of us
sometimes think,
although we feel
it is wrong.

Kuldeep Kaur

I WANT TO ...

I want to fly like a bird
1Not to know what is freedom
But to experience new heights
I want to die like a soldier
Not to know what is martyrdom
But to see the glory in death

I want to blossom like a flower
Not to know what is fragrance
But to understand HIS beautiful creation
I want to stand like a rock in the sea
Not to know what is endurance
But to learn what it takes to be there.

I want to help the poor and weak
Not to know what is charity
But to realise what it means to be privileged.
I want to tread the path of a legend
Not to know what is immortality
But to assimilate the essence of aspiration and sacrifice.

Larry Jaffe

ALWAYS READY TO FIGHT

You are always ready to fight my cousin.
I grew up learning how not to fight how to
Never be in contention never confront anything
for fear of reprisal. I grew up to be a shadow
my cousin. To never put any foot forward lest
it be the wrong foot. A wallflower is what I was
taught was the best position for manhood to live and
thrive. To never right wrongs and never fight
someone else's battles and they were all
someone else's battles. I was taught to hide
the chips on my shoulders and never be seen
I was taught to be a shadow my cousin and having
patience "this too shall pass." Only the angel
of death has stopped passing my cousin. And
I wonder who really wins these battles that
pause at the tips of blind bayonets.
I can hear mother's screams and I wonder why
you don't say Kaddish for my relatives when
I sit Shiva for yours. This disturbs me greatly.
If you are going to condemn death then you
must condemn death for all, not just your side.
Violence is a plague that riddles our civilization
moreover, makes it bleed from dawn to dusk. Why must
you suicide your bombers into my children, why
must my tanks roll over yours? I ask who builds bombs
who builds tanks? who benefits from this hate and
retribution my cousin? I sit in anguish, I do not know
whom to believe so I believe no one. There is no violence
there is no hate, I tell myself but refuse to listen. It is all
violence and all hate. And I know it is neither. You say

You love me. If this is so tell your relatives to be quiet.
Tell them to shut the fuck up and I will do the same
with mine!

FINGERS FIRST TOUCHING

She has heard
all the clichés
of warmth
and persuasion.
She has lived
all the moments
of instant anything
and survived it all.
Then there was
the moment
of eyes first seeing and
fingers first touching
in transparent overture.
It is that first touch
that awakens loneliness
arousing memories
long forgotten
mystifying wonder.
A flash of connection
a clash of indifference
then silence
the loneliness
in poignant scream
of eyes first meeting
elation and woe
in single gasp.
He worries
she might lose
her virginity to ancestors
or herself
that she might
forget the smile
that fingers touch.

Lauren Diane Ovsevitz

WORLD OF DREAMS

I wonder what its like to live in a World of Dreams
where everything around you is not what it seems.
Where waterfalls turn into dunes of sand
where seagulls transformed into rubber bands.
The sky seems blue, but soon turns pink
where rivers run colors of rainbow ink.
I wonder what its like to live in a World of Dreams
where hideous dragons have golden wings.
Where monsters are the nicest creatures
and beauties have monstrous features.
The fairies would bite and maim
while lions act oh so tame.
I wonder what its like to live in a World of Dreams
where rain clouds are made of strawberry creams.
Where lightening spreads gold all around
where a sparrows song is a horrid sound.
The goblins would smile and smirk
while the unicorns would plot and lurk.
I wonder what its like to live in a World of Dreams.
Would you be able to figure out what every thing means?

Len Rely

THE WHITE BAT

Aha! The long-eared vixen comes to grace this clammy cave.
The cricket from his bower strums and cobwebs gently wave.
Among these merry floating moths and shifting stalags be,
all in all and with a wingless fall come thou to me.
The paleness of your color shames the Moon we both adore.
The nighthawk sings of silken things that call you to my shore.
I've waited in this crevice for a dark eternity,
my outstretched wings await you, come thou, come thou! unto me.

Les Wicks

JERUSALEM TRACK

The smoke has become
another season.
An element.
It's collecting around the trees making
their leaves seem weighted, a curve
in that trunk suggesting recoil but
everything is just
doing the business as I walk through a forest
that's anticipating the coming
feast of fire under a chanting mat of cicadas.
Elsewhere flames explode on touch
rich eucalypt oils,
minute white flowers lost in a sunburst.
Will my season end so
dark smudged & furious? Perhaps
there is no alternative
- summers never surrender -
it's always declared war against heat
by an undermining wind as the world turns over
to warm its other half.
I write this as I sit
on an outcrop looking down at the Hawkesbury
watching the young man climbing the slope
(so much energy,
spraying uselessly).

Turn see an old man behind,
not embarrassed to be caught in his thoughts over me.
So we too are seasons.
We too are smoke. Free & inevitable.

Ackn: *The Ways of Waves*

LeVaughn Flynn

THE TRUTH

If you could look in my eyes
And see my soul.
If you could read my lips
And hear my cries.
If you could take a journey through me
With my embrace.
If my footsteps left memos
That could only be interpreted by the unfeigned.
If only you could do these,
Then, you would know who I am.

Lee R. Lowder III

BUTTERFLY KISSES

Butterfly kisses, soft sincere
Whispering 'I Love You' in your ear
Warm embrace, soft gentle touch
A look of the eye that means so much
A kiss as soft as snow in the air
A way to show how much I care
A touch of the hand, a wink of the eye
Hint of your lips cause a wistful sigh
Not a word spoken, but so much is said
With just a tender kiss upon your head
For your desire, to fulfill your wishes
I send to you my butterfly kisses.

Lee Ennis

MY CAPTAIN WAS LOST AT SEA

Abandon ship, the end is near
She'll soon be going down I fear
We've done all that we could do
Far out here on the ocean blue
Man the lifeboats, do it now
I hope to save them all somehow
Darkness will be upon us soon
I wait for my impending doom
Hurry now you must make haste
I wish for not one life to waste
At the ships wheel is where I'll be
Let no one come to look for me
It shall be known I'm lost at sea
My place is with this grand lady
A captain's life is never done
As we become the setting sun

YOU ARE BEAUTY

You are the first flower in spring
You are the warmth at winter's end
The taste of sweet
You are the angel that appears in dream
A symphony to the ear
Yes the music of the gods

You are life with all of its glorious wonders
You are beauty
I look at you and my heart aches from want
You are beauty
An amazing gift to time, to earth
When men speak of beauty they speak of you
You take my breath
You are beauty.

Lisa M. Lewis

IF I

If I look into your eyes,
a mere mortal
and expect to see salvation there

I might as well walk, barefoot
Through the broken glass of uncertainty
And not expect to open a vein

If I grasp at the beating of a heart,
Human as my own
And expect a Mother's touch

I might as well take the joy
From my reborn soul
And throw it to the wind
Before it can cry out to live

If I take your word as gold
and try to hold it's value to my heart
I might as well cast the worthless pennies
To everyone with outstretched hands....

Lisa-Marie Griffin

I'LL NEVER FORGET

In the tender hours;
of the pre-dawn light
I dream of you;
I it seems so right.

The morning dew;
touched by rain
your laughter fades;
to a brand new day.

Lowell Damron

SEARCHING THE INSANITY

Sanity runs along a jagged line
in my mind
It wishes to break free
but something within me
will not let it find
a way out of the insanity
I can feel it
searching for reality
In a world as confused as it is
I can feel it searching
searching for comfort
reaching out
trying to grasp hope
in a world full of hate
Sanity will not escape
this mind of mine
It is trapped
deep behind
all that is left
of my reality.

Louise P. Saltkill

PROMISE

Promise that you'll love me forever and a day.
For I can't bear to think the thought that you might go away.
Promise that you'll be there every step of the way.
For I can't stand nor walk alone, I need you here today.
Promise that you'll shine on me, From the heavens above my dear.
For I can no longer see your face in the crowd,
Just your loveliness, Wish you were here.
Promise that you'll welcome me,
When I walk through those pearly gates,
and take my hand, help me understand, the path we know as fate.
Promise that I'll never forget...
Your love, your grace, your voice, your face.
I promise that I'll that I'll the live the fullest, and honor your sweet name.

Lucretia Ann Campos

JESUS AND THE BUDDHA

Jesus and the Buddha standing hand in hand
Both bringing rays of hope to all foreign lands
With humble lessons of truth, peace, and wisdom
Meant for all of us regardless where we're from
So why can't the leaders of our confused world
See there is no need for the stones we all hurl?

Luis Cabalquinto

THE DAY AFTER
(for Sean Lugano, who died in the WTC horror of September 11)

This morning, outside
my window,
the light is just
right on an oak
branch, leaves
moving
in the wind
just so —

as if
no tower burned
and fell, nor any
human died.

What this is
really saying
though:
it's now upon us,
left to live,
to move on —

with the wind's laughter,
with the kindness of leaves,
with the heart's undying light —

each given day —

as if they
have not hated us
and you have not
too early died.

IN ANOTHER COUNTRY

On the fast-moving
train from Barcelona
to Madrid, thoughts

of home drift in
and out of me
like smoke from someone

next door burning
a pile of dry leaves
in the late afternoon.

This afternoon Spain
takes the color and scent
of burning leaves.

Mandy Dyer

DEFLATED

Deflated
Beneath a grey cloud
Dodging the downpour
Of my emotional tribulation
Affliction
Needing to work through my
dejection
My trial of
Sadness
Of what I have come to know.
Sorrow
Felt from a list of promises
So meaningless
Barren
Left from words so unprolific
Solitude
In my emotional state
Retired so abruptly
Now living my life within a broken
Bubble
Emotions seeping through the minute
Holes
Meeting up to face the reality
To learn again to become
Total within myself.

Marek Lugowski

& WHEN THE TEA EBBS

& when the tea ebbs
& when the happyfeet inherit the mirth — sandy
shoals of fjord or firth or prairie

then

some dazzling things yes! some dazzling things!
await in algae on the beaches — secondary gifts —
amber set in silver — scat of boozeglass — and
del monte's darkly hollow cans of shaven peaches.

Maria Cristina Azcona

ANGEL'S VOICE

Impredictable mystery of wings
disrupt sorrowful darkness.
Slowly a butterfly trembles
while moonlight begins a dance.

Today, the Heyday of angels in advance,
give us an admonitory command.
Humanhood's selfishness must end at once.

Unbelievable sense of a third dimension
grows inside the thoughts of freedom.
A voice, lovely and caressing demands attention
while a golden feather floates and reaches depths.

Finally an awareness of the Lord
fills the empty edifice of soul.
Internal wisdom is increasing.
Compassion is the way... and everybody
listens now their old internal Angel's voice.

Maria Theresa Ib

59° LATITUDE N

No place for Pele this, no
heat-scarred ash here for her
to raise her hell from. Cold
stains the mind, callouses
the heart. This iron tropic's
sick with slow matter. Yet
spleen's slit wrist seethes
beneath its skin, vikings
up the people, makes them
durable.

Marie

THE MUSE

The Muse
She cast her spell
And I
So quickly fell
For her
Smile so sweet
No one
Could ever meet
Her depth
And honor true
Granting
To none but you
The words
From worlds above
A gift
To you with love
From the
Sweet Muse that's yours
From She
Who opens doors
To those
Places unknown
Heavens
From which are flown
The words
For which you crave
The Muse

Makes you her slave
Whispers
Within your mind
Whispers
However kind
The words
She will always send
From birth
Until your end
Echoes
Within your head
Torture
While in your bed
The Muse
Won't let you sleep
It's hers
Whose life you keep
It's hers
Whose words you write
It's her
Who gives you light
Into
The world unknown
From which
Your words have grown...
To She
Who'll always be
The one
Woman for me
Prophet
Talking through God
A gift
To me from God.

Marie Guay

BECAUSE OF ME BECAUSE OF HIM

On a tree they killed my king.
My sins caused Him hanging
In misery, crying out to His Father.
The soldiers did not bother
Caring what he said when he forgave.
But I did and now must be brave
To live every day for Him.
Although I fail and fall into sin
At times,
I dwell not on my crimes.

Because I still remember:
They were blowing hard,
The winds that spring day.

I looked up, he smiled
Down on me His pardon.
My sins were washed away
when on that cross, death He defied.

Marki Twain

EAST AND WEST

    The sun rose on the East today and also on the west,
    God made the sun to shine on the East and also on the West.
    The Moon rose on the East tonight and also on the West,
    God made the moon to shine on the East and also on the West.
    God cries when children die in the East and also in the West,
    God made the Earth a whole not just East and West.
    God wants Water, Food and Medicine shared,
    in the East and also in the West.
    if not,
    God can take the light away,
    from the East and also the West.

THE GOLDEN WINGS

    The golden wings of Angels fly up in the sky,
    guiding souls of children to Heaven when they die.
    The golden wings of Angels hover in the sky,
    watching the souls of people suffering as they cry.
    The golden wings of Angels sadly hover in the sky,
    above the armies of all men, wondering why?
    The golden wings of Angels shine from Gods pure love
    for all His Earthly children as He watches from above.

Martin A Enticknap

FOOTSTEPS OF GAIA

There can be no more time for tears,
No more mopping the brow and wringing hands for the dead.
In her footsteps you can see the potential,
The power that is yours to wield in the making of a new thread.

Allow the call that is seeping up from the earth,
To bathe your hands in the soil and feel the wisdom that she demands.
That you become the footsteps that she has shown you,
To stand tall against those coming to turn the fields blood red.

The silence is only the beginning in the debt you owe,
No more idle hands but the threads that you are ordained to be.
In the weave that is your strength to be the banner,
That will fly in the face of the walking dead.

Your life is bound to every footstep she takes,
When she bleeds you shall bleed.
Her wounds are your wounds,
When she dies you die too.

So it is written, so it shall be done...
So the steps begin...

Mary Kathryn Cannon

OUR TEARS HE WIPES

How many a tear more must we shed
I've about lost count somewhere
For soon as we wipe those from our eyes
there are always more trials to bear

If it wasn't for the grace of God
that he gives to us each day
We wouldn't be able to withstand the tests
that comes all kinds of ways

There are times we have no thought at all
to just what each day may bring
But better still maybe it's for the best
for even a little hurt will sting

Sometimes you try to do all you can
to make sure the day goes right
But still in all we know we must be tried
so we grit our teeth and hold on tight

But soon one day we'll hear God say
I've come to wipe your tears
and this is your day to rejoice for a while
so put aside your worries and fears.

Matthew Johnson

THE CALM

And so I sit,
On this lonely rock,
It's the only thing that's dry.
And I stare unto,
The rippled glass,
It makes me want to cry.

Then I walk,
In my solitude,
I stare unto the sky,
This tree sees me,
With crooked eyes,
He says I can't deny.

Oh i,
I just want to fly
Above this wretched soul
Oh i,
I just want to fly,
Fly away from it all.

Unto the open sea,
Through and above the naked clouds,
Spaced between the waves of eternity,
We'll sleep.

Melisande Luna

DAUGHTER

Snake gave Eve:
serpentine thoughts,
cherry plum hips,
opposable thumbs.

She plucked nectarines
burgeoning on boughs;
a flora of fruitful sins.

Ripe peach proffered,
bloomed between thighs.
She sighed, ecstasy,
a blossom on the tip
of asp's wicked tongue.

MercyRain

EMPTY HANDS

dark water ricochets slow off the old pier
lapping sad — mortuary of flesh
fish drowned, diseased
and another day and I'm still alone...
where was I when you needed me so?
hiding in needles, in aromas of sanctity
left all alone, you're gone now... past

look at my hands, bare and empty —
they lust the razor lines of blood
that sharp incessant pain of forgiveness...

Michael D. Petti

ABSENCE

I wait
in expectation
of your crackling consciousness
to break this ominous suspension
of my heart

a smell upon the air
the ozone of loneliness
thick, pervades
senses, aroused for darkness
coagulates my despair

inhaling a day
turned night with
bird-abandoned trees
splintering the earth
all sap drained

leeched of life
I draw upon all withered things
for acceptance
understanding, beneath
a gray, still sky

silence is
the nourishment of your world
a blood-scented storm
promising only the calm
death-like, in its arrival.

Michael J Shepard

ISOLATION

All alone.
Hidden in a world
That's spiteful.
Evil
Surrounds me.
And bounds me
To hell.
I'm sinking.
I'm drowning
In the middle
Of a sea of sorrow.
It's sorrow
Only from me
And only for me.
I'm alone.

And the world
Passes me by.
I'm lost now.
In retrospect
I guess I've always been lost.
Wading through
Social disorder,
Neglected,
I wait for
The ravages of the world
To consume me,

And tear me
Limb from limb.
I expect it.
I want it.
I know nothing else.
I'm alone.

Befriended.
Betrayed.
The difference grows vague.
Confusion
Leads to
The acceptance of pain.
I suffer
The ways of the world.
It's hell.
It's twisted.
It's crooked.
Completely fucked up.
I'm broken.
I'm fixed.
I don't know which.
There's no one
To help me.
To tell me
Who I am.
Nobody cares.
I'm alone.

Michael Levy

I AM THE ONE

I am the discreet whispers on the breeze.
Listen to my voice as it brushes your delicate cheek,
I am all you think - all you seem - all you contemplate,
My thoughts are etched in every rock

Through eons of years I have called your name,
No replies have been heard, no true purpose found,
Listen to my voice as it sails upon the wind,
You need to know my message - to find authentic meaning.

As I float on by your mind - be aware,
You know I am around you,
Yet you will not listen to my voice
Could it be your choice is not of your choosing?

I am your own true self dear one,
I have been here forever and a day,
Will you suffer in your illusion - endure rather than enjoy,
Or will you becalm your mind -become aware of my timeless silent voice,

Michael R. Collings

CONTINUITY

The river passes, gurgling its thoughts
beneath the level of my comprehension.
I think I know the spot, the shore, the awkward twist of branch
on the dead oak just across the glimmer-
I feel I know the spot, the shadow,
the whitened air cascading with small puffs from cottonwoods.

It seems familiar-and yet I know that while all else
seems familiar, while the river passes
unimpeded, uninterrupted,
I see it for the first time
and the last
precisely thus-as molecules from far distant
foreignnesses slip by-
infinitude of molecules I have never greeted,
never known, never seen
and never will-
and yet it seems I think I know the spot.

The twist of oak is not the same.
A flake of drying bark has shivered from its branch.
A sparrow snapped a single twig
to help construct a nest, perhaps, since last
I stood by this small stone, itself
transformed by grit swept past.
One dangling leaf surviving from its green-time

might have tumbled to the earth to hide itself
in humus thick below.
And so, the twist is not the same,
and yet it seems I know that branch.

And the air, rife with cotton just as last time,
yet not the same, not just, but altered with each second
each breath of mine and wind that whirls
across the river's dimpled whorls.
Not just the same
and yet it seems I know the air,
have breathed this air and watched this air before.
And so it goes. All changes. All remains
unalterably the same, perhaps, within the tumult
of imagination. And somewhere, trapped beneath
familiarity and essential foreign-ness,
between what seems and is,
the river is the same, the oak endures,
the flagrant tufts of aging white
have been and are and will remain and
I think I know this spot and do.

Michael Paul Chmielecki

SLEEPLESSNESS

lack of sleep
is a muscle made
of black threads,
ember eyes.

you stitch them to
a pillow case,
unable to feel
the powdered sand.

your hands close over
the loneliest body,
the honeyed taste
of broken bread.

your imprints imbibe
empty moments
to wonder why
she's not here.

was she ever?
close your eyes.
imagine the embers.
rose-laid sand.

Michelle Dunk-Martin

UNDECIDED

Unable to decide
The answer right in front of my face
You lean over just enough to confuse things
I lay my head down
Only to hear your heartbeat
Only to smell your scent
Only to taste your truth
You loved her
While I loved you
Answers need to be given
Broken promises need to be fixed
I'm unable to decide
The answer now
Is a mist of confusion
In your eyes and mine.

Mike Subritzky

THE OPEN WINDOW

Through the open window
across the meadow green
and down beside the river bank
I drift at night in dream.

Where willows sweep the water
and birdsong fills the air
the morning sunlight greets me
with wild flowers everywhere.

A fat jack trout for breakfast
and a brew of billy tea
the smell of burning wood smoke
that's where I long to be.

So give me some more dreamtime
and I'll drift back there once more
to a time of endless sunshine
before the Vietnam war.

Mukunda Tom Stiles

THE WAY TO OHIO

On the way through Ohio
Maxfield Parish
interrupted the journey
to pastel the sky.

I stop and he changes his
brush
to paint the proud sky dancer
streaking Ribbons
beyond Her,
lighting the sky.

Whites so white
they are crystalline.
Blues so blue they
reach eternity.

The door closes —
back to
the drive.

Natasha C. Burroughs

SILENT LOVE

As we sit and talk, I realize you are writing upon my heart
Words vibrant with warmth
As it ignites my soul into an eternal flame of desire.. for you
To share my life, and treasured moments
Amazing how I've spent so many days with you
But only today have I found that you are the one
The one I needed the most
How could I be so blinded by other things
I know remember when I cried to sleep because he hurt me again
You rubbed my brow, and kissed my face, and listened
As you spoke softly...choose me
I think on the moment when things were fallin' apart
You hugged me so tight, even made 'em right
As you looked to my innermost and said why not choose me?
Then tragedy came, hurt so unbearable and unspeakable
Again, you were there. This time I listened to you
Never really heard what you were saying before
But I came to you as I were, Tattered and bruised
Never knew you cared so much
Until we sat and talked
You wrote on my heart that day
"For I am God, I will never leave nor forsake you, even until the end of the world"
That day i read what you wrote
Finally heard and accepted. The beginning of our own Love affair.

Nguyen Duc Batngan

WHITE BONES

Let's assume me to be a spoilt child, Mother
For not fulfilling Father's former career
not mature yet finding my life blindly drifting away
When today is it light or dark?

Regard me as having been dead, Mother.
Since the first moment you saw me off crying
On my forehead your fragrance still lingering
So affectionate as the merciful Holy Mother.

Forget me as the once lost homeland
Though on Father's head the hair has turned white.
There's still, in this strange land, the same tinge of home's familiar clouds
So how can I pull back the waning moon?

Let's assume it to be like flowing water, Mother
Or as I had not been born
Wrecked and lost nights are followed by days of sadness and shame
The grief swayed along the shady white of the dark soul

Now I am in exile, Mother
And then my white bones will be left in a strange place
Send my words to Father, please Mother
That hard as it is, I still hold a smile.

Nicholas Gallimore

HEARTBROKEN

My heart is aching
for your tender love.
The pain cant stop aching
without your tender loving care.
Give me your love that's
was the phrase you told me.
Now that I did am here all alone.
Waiting and calling out your name.
My body tense when I see you in the arms of another.
Tears rushed down my eyes the day you told me
you weren't in love with me.
I thought you love me but you
just lead me on to tears.

Nilanshu Kumar Agrawal

FRENZY OF FLESH

Exhaustive frenzy of flesh
Scorching fire of senses
Digital obscenity of laptop
Reminding the dull poet
Of the dance of Corpses
With the reptiles.

Olaf Korder

DATE

his voice really had such a boyish tone
that almost scorched my telephone
we made an appointment for half past eight
so now I am waiting for my date
in a downtown bar I happen to know
with fifteen minutes or more to go.

someone enters and shuts the door
would that be him, did we speak before?
by the time I order my third glass of beer
it's really getting crowded in here
two girls giggling, screaming with laughter
students behaving increasingly dafter

meanwhile the clock shows way past ten
I decide I've done tonight with men
I scorn myself for being so blind
till he has finally left my mind.

Olukoga Tayo

BREEZE

    How cool and largesse is the breeze
    After the creaking noise of the
    Roof during the day
    When the sun has gone to bed
    From the boiling face of the earth
    Where it comes from no one knows
    Where it goes to no one knows
    How cool and largesse is the breeze
    An unseen comforter
    Sneaking through the window blind
    To the living room
    Making a cloister place to be
    It comes and cajoles the trees in the forest
    Out of sadness
    Giving happiness to the plants of the garden
    Messenger of the comforter
    Swift at times, slow at times
    Harbinger of an eventide.

Padmore Agbemabiese

ALONE
(to Keats: la belle dame sans merci)

born many days away
from my birthday
doctors gave me
ten days to live

like water gathering like a lake
on an island
grandma cried in intervening silence

she bent over me
held my lips to her breast
killing many owls in my dreams

like palms walking with fronds
to reach out to heaven
grandma in the village spread her wings
before soaring waves cross my path

it is thirty birthdays since
grandma in the village spread her wings
like cabbage is no vegetable
no one counts me as alive
'and this is why
I sojourn here alone
palely loitering
with my sledge whither'd from lakes'

IN MEMORIAM

if you want to remember me
remember the raindrops of tonight
the sheet of darkness engulfing our frame
the floating stars creating mirrors
that ripple smiles at our touch
the chorus of crickets chanting
all weave a wave
like a pencil-tip bending lines
into our dreams
just remember all this
and my name will not be lost
among the used-up cinders
dumped in the dust-side
of forgotten memory.

Page Malbrough

THE CHASE

Breath is about to run out.
Drops out of every shriveled toe, hurdles
each knee-knob and dashes into the sagging belly.
She jolts as if waking from a bad dream and sees herself

ahead with the final blast of the bellows.
Out sails the child inside daddy's corner store. The door
shudders against the gust and whip of the windy city.
Her knit hat rims the eyes, its tassel dangles.
Standing straight as glass bottles

she waits to be lifted and carried off.
Out sails a wife, lips and eyebrows drawn dark,
in her mink stole and leather gloves she flares fingers
outstretched the baby clinging to his husky
maw in the sweep of the second story window

the bonnet slipping off in their scuffle.
Out sails the grandmother her apron tied beneath
the crook of her spine, cradles her darling
who was not to touch the hot stove but blisters

earned not learned, blossom from a fertile mind.
She wells out cool air in the span of time her lungs allow.
The pain disappears before passing into a breath
a funnel of cloud, a vanishing of footsteps.

Pat Phillips West

FIRSTS AND NEVERS

    The man who first called her princess
never saw her float down the stairs
on prom night
The man who celebrated her
every achievement
never read her college acceptance letter
honors at entrance
The man who taught her to drive
never saw her first car
The man who taught her to laugh
never had a chance to witness
her humor become like his own
The man who applauded her
first and loudest
never had the opportunity to attend
her staring roles
The man who loved her first
never met her first love
The man who kissed away her
first tear
never imagined
her deepest sorrow.

Patricia Gomes

REUNION

I planned to call you
I must have
I remember picking up the phone
punching in a familiar number...

I planned to call you
I think I did
I may have gotten the machine,
lost my nerve before the beep.

I planned to call you
Really...
at least a thousand times
You answered once, didn't you?
I was the silence.

Patricia H. Regensburg

BACKWARD GLANCES

I wander backward through my mind
to look for treasures and I find
just shadows lurking all about
the growing mountain of my doubt
that searching will make age concede
to tangled thoughts and crushing need.
How gratifying it would be
to thumb my nose at certainty
and find those minute misplaced cells
wherein lost information dwells
instead of wild lamenting on
the times, the names, the dates all gone.
I hope in my next life to know
that in whatever form I grow
I'll not recall a single tear,
not even childhood's smallest fear,
but only feel the fever of
whatever laughter, fun and love
will help alleviate the pain
of stumbling through a life again.

Patricia Wellingham-Jones

CHOICES

Colon, Panama: the armpit of the world,
you assure me in scribbled notes
you send from your tied-up boat. Day by day
you grow weaker in your self-imposed solitude.
The mahogany decks you scraped,
sanded and varnished, then
scraped, sanded and varnished
all over again. The brass rails
throwing the tropical sun back in its face.
The galley you fitted out with real crystal
safe behind brackets, china a newlywed
would covet for her first home.
You, who sailed the world's seas,
now moored to a dock trapping unwary feet
in its rot, air thick with the stink
of decayed fish and vomit, on a harbor
you pray you never fall into.

You tried it here, saw the doctors, held down
a job that streaked your eyes red then fled
back to your dream in southern waters. Somehow,
amid that sun-blistered deck, the sails striped
with mold and torn, the finger-smeared brass,
you see coconut palms bending over a beach,
the sparkle of shells, mermaids swift

in a clear blue-green sea. You sip rum
from chipped crystal, tune out
the curses, hear trade winds instead, regard
skinny toes turning blue below wasted legs.
Your long sigh—broken by TB-cough—
from a deep well of contentment
reaches me, still not understanding,
here at home.

UNSTERILE ENVIRONMENT

Around the globe the wind swirls
in soft gusts and monsoons carrying particles
of the quick and the dead
to our lungs, into our cells,
making us all, as long as we live—
and thereafter—part of each other.

We all breathe—no exceptions—recycled air:
nomad's sweat swept on a desert wind, bull elks
panting in the clash of rut, the last squawk
of a chicken caught in owl talons, a sick
old man's groan. And star jasmine wafting
on a summer night, pine branches broken under snow,
a packed-diapered baby's howl of rage.

I smile at the new mother
who wraps her infant against the warm breeze,
double-boils his bottles of water,
wards off big family kisses,
as if the baby weren't already
inhaling the second-hand breath of the world.

MRS. COYOTE

Town knows her
as Mrs. Coyote. Tall and lean,
she lopes through Gold Rush Country
in tawny sweaters with earth
stained pants, her sharp nose
twitching in thought.
Grieved by the western habit
of draping coyote carcasses
over fence posts, unconvinced
their marauding brothers
get the hint, her main concern
is the wildness in their cells.
She sees these untamed eyes
staring out of poets.
Poets, who must be left undisturbed
to record the unwritten songs
that rustle dry grass,
whip treetops into leaf storms,
frenzy incoming tides.
Who express the wildness
in cells stifled long.

R.A.Munoz

MONKEY

Little monkey, powder monkey, tickling my toes
She knows I am yearning - just another dose

My head is swimming, sweet ache my friend
Let a little snow fall, what a pretty way to end

The daily grind an obstacle, my walk always a mile
Line it up, cook it up, baby it's time to smile

Rubies on my lips, does this child look gay
If only momentarily satisfied, what more is there to say?

Richard James Allen

NO SURRENDER

Faith is flimsy
in the face of
death, madness, war

but inside us
it burns
like little fires.

Be terrified
of the glow
in our eyes.

Richard Paul Crowther

MUSINGS

Compassion compensates for the dark and grim,
In the glass the liquid, your lips around the rim,
Growing pains, aging pains, all are the same,
Wishing evil would return from whence it came,
We try, all sorts of tears we cry, not knowing why,
Just knowing it hurts, waiting for a humane Magi,
Holding your breath, fighting your days, heart on sleeve,
Heart on fire, head so tired, put aside your need,
Spend some money, claw some honey, be funny,
Jump around, cause some sound, leave the ground,
Come back down, don't be a clown, you're a noun,
Not a verb, you're set in your way, never to stray,
Path set, mind set, destiny is your true calling,
Look up, fly, look down, soon be sinking, falling,
Look to the world, evil atrocities too appalling,
Only those on the news, many limited views,
Only we see where there are camera crews,
Shiver, sent up your spine, then you're fine,
Look over shoulder, just ignore the crime.
Human compassion, a gift and a burden,
Human rights, needs to be an obligation,
Don't speak to me, speak to them, listen to yourself,
Change is constant, people born and die,
Sometimes sudden, sometimes by stealth,
For life we don't need divine navigation,
People try, speak their mind true, we curse them,
Hush now, calm yourselves, don't cry.

Richard Stevenson

JACKIE BATTLE

After Marguerite left me
Jackie and I became a team.
I saw other women sometimes,
but she was my main squeeze.
Jackie put up with a lot too.
I put her through her paces.
Mostly it was the cocaine,
my paranoia and mood swings.
Sometimes it got real crazy.
I'd take seven or eight Tuinals
after snorting cocaine all day,
start to talk to the walls.
Then Jackie and my sister
found these polaroid snaps
of naked women I'd taken.
They totally freaked on me.
The women played me like a trumpet
and got it on in kinky ways
that'd get me all charged up.
We would snort and play together.
Man, that was some shit storm
I weathered over that one!
It cost me another relationship –
one I regret losing to this day.
Jackie holed up in her apartment,
pulled the phone jack from the wall.

She wouldn't talk to me at all.
Then I broke my friggin' ankles.
I had gotten high, went out after hours,
crashed my Lambourghini
into a median in the highway
when I fell asleep at the wheel.
Another fix I got myself in, Ollie –
I was months recovering, still craved coke.
Even took off with Jim Rose one day –
and Jackie hung up the phone for good.
I was in a dark hole in those days.
People looked on my sorry ass
the way they did when I
was usin' junk and pimpin'.
I was some piece of work.
Didn't get to the bottom
of that cold black hole
for some time afterward.
So, yeah, Jackie was aptly named.
She certainly had an uphill battle
with me. She endured every indignity
before gettin' her ass free.
I didn't have my jones
to talk to on the phone,
but I was some long distance
motherfucker in my bones.

Rickey K. Hood

CURIO

There is a crack on the hard wood floor
near the corner where the curio cabinet holds pictures
of my family, precious little things,
nic-nacs I've collected over the years
a life now dulled from dust and neglect

I've been busy
making a world for myself
busy/ tearing down the old and making way for the new
creating a place for me
renovating, remolding my world
my life

all was going to plan until
I noticed a crack on the hard wood floor
near the corner where the curio cabinet sits
and I saw what I had been destroying

so what now?
my new world is nearly complete
should I rip up this crack and every thing with it
or open the curio and dust off the memories

to keep my world
undone.

SITTING ON A BENCH IN THE PARK

A cool spring afternoon
soft breezes making reflective
ripples on the man made pond
a pond encircled by fishers.
there is a rhythm to the casting and reeling
casting and reeling/
casting and reeling
of their polls and lines
patiently waiting for a soft nibble
to jerk in the hook and reel in the catch

ducks, geese and mallards float relaxed
on the ripples
stealing bait meant for the fish.
others glide on the warm breeze chasing or swooping
on unsuspecting insects

the air here is free to move
not confined between avenues, boulevards, and parkways
it has the perfume of the pines and cedars, oaks and grass
the green things
this air is free to breathe
the lovers of this place come often
just to walk around it's man made pond
and slowly take-in 'the green things' and feel human
to feed the ducks,
or just sit patiently fishing
waiting for a nibble.

Rina Ferrarelli

EMIGRANT/IMMIGRANT II

A slight accent.
Forming
each phrase before
delivery
and never a slur.

Checking
every move,
prepared
for all contingencies,
Close
yet not quiet.

Insisting
on a knife and fork
when your fingers
would so as well.

Almost there.
The place sighted,
but out of reach.
Destined never to cross

into the interior.
A bridge, a border town.

Robert Edgar Burns

THANKS TO MY FRIENDS !

To all my friends who write me,
And are now like family,
I want to tell you thank you,
You, make me happy as can be.

I have diabetes,
And a poorly working heart.
I was forced to retire,
From a job I didn't want to part.

I'm in and out of the hospital.
I just got home again today.
I don't know how much longer,
The Lord shall let me stay.

The pain I'm in is staggering.
I never knew it could be this bad.
But my spirit gets so much brighter,
With all your words for they make me glad.

For there is power in the written word,
If it comes from a persons heart.
It can heal and mend a wounded soul,
As you've done for me from the start.

I really love to read your words,
But often times I don't reply.

It's not that I don't wish to,
But exhaustion seems to always stop by.

So If you think I'm ignoring you,
Nothing's farther from the truth.
I'd like to name each one of you,
And thank you all at a kissing booth.

Thank you all for thinking of me,
And the wonderful things you say.
If wealth is measured by friendships,
Then I'm the luckiest man alive today!

Robert L. Jackson

FROM A SOFT WORLD
(Taken from Dry Holy Land: Memoirs of Israel)

My clothing dries
outside the apartment window,
hardening to a crisp
around a wire.
My skin itches
revealing the softness
of artificial scars
and superficial stories.
I spend money
on a textured vacation
in hopes to inscribe myself
with those not so bland.
I spend money
freely on souvenirs,
not being swindled,
but releasing my silver bubble.
My clothing dries,
revealing an altered fabric,
untarnished
but with an altered gleam.

Rodney Kuhn

MARIONETTE

The day dawned bright and clear where I set,
The time was passed with precious Marionette
She never said a word and I was there to hear,
Everyone else was afraid but I had nothing to fear
She was the most beautiful from all the others,
Set apart from youth, even from her brothers
Why I found her and loved her like I do, I'm not sure,
All I knew was that my love was reserved only for her
Maybe it was from the very look in her eyes,
Or maybe it was because everything in life dies
I had no one else and she was there by herself,
I just didn't have the heart to leave her on the shelf
The day dawned clear and bright with a steady rain,
And I always hide my face whenever I'm in pain
Nobody cares enough and life is a broken dream,
This doll made of wood and strings is nothing like it seems
I hold her close enough and she knows that I'm alone,
She will follow me in death as history has shown
The time dies again and I care enough to forget,
But my heart remains broken as I sit alone with Marionette.

Roland Leach

EPIPHANY IN THE DESERT

Christ went into the desert
the solitude of stone
a cold night sky

gods only inhabit the desert & sea
you wont find them in cities & towns
they don't like crowds

preferring moonlight on water
the sands cooling down

a place where it is one-on-one
face to face
choose your weapon

so Christ went into the desert
armed with silence
What does a carpenter see in the stars?

how can you imagine the night sky
before Einstein & Galileo
the thought of infinity
the millions of miles
where stars had already died
light years away

some say Satan appeared at this moment
tempting a famished Christ

telling him that a sonofgod
could feed himself
turning stones to bread

and it was here in a night desert
where he had gone with silence
that he saw the sky for what it was
pinpoints of eternity
the quantum being that existed
and didn't
feeding himself with the vision

before returning to galilee
as thin as hunger
as wild as love.

Rolland G. Smith

SPIRIT DIVER

I saw my soul before its birth
Upon an image deep in space
And dove, from high, down to the earth
To breathe again the breath of race.

Through a tunnel I did steal
Into a womb of warmth and love.
A strange forgetting I did feel
While on the passage from above.

My leap was silent 'til my cry-
Awakening in birthing strife-
That must be when I said goodbye
And died into the new of life.

When I awoke with earthly breath
And density to comprehend,
I knew that birth is like a death,
Each is the same, there is no end.

Romus Simpson

I THOUGHT OF YOU

it was a blue dusk
an empty park marbled in shadows
the broad luminous back of the sun striding
leaving without bells to another early country
& the moon not yet awake
stirring love above the night hand canopy
god began to finger the nightly fresco of stars
that shone like eyes in the lake's late swan reflections
a bird shook a streetlight awake
then by the shrill iron gates of the echoing cathedral
two women prayed another lit
wandering there
in the vague halo of the central California dusk
i thought of you

in the meridian of late dusk where the moon comes
behind the sentinel crows that are the first deep night
an orange silver river of memory burned
with the remnants of the brown October day
pushing north to the stars & into greater breath
i moved along the city's weary eye
caught gold in the avenue river rushes
was alone where each bare blind tree etched Arabic at the moon
listened to leaves flute & whirl in my wake
& thought of you

Ron Cole

INFIELD FLY RULE

I remember the April heat wave
how it tantalized young growing buds
confused their growth.

Down at the local park
a group of young girls – 12 & 13
squat bend twist and jump
in an effort to capture
a soft white ball
that whimsically comes their way.

The April sky flourishes in heat
too young, though
to cross its own line of maturity
instead it ventures into fantasy.

Poised on first and second
the runners squint in April heat
as eyes trace the crack of a bat,
but the soft white ball lingers too long
and becomes lost in the dying sun.

The game is over, so the umpire says
the final out forgotten in April's short suspense,

and the girls walk home dejectedly
towards what may have been,

If only, they feel
if only, April would never end.

Rosa M. DelVecchio

A THUNDERING SILENCE

God gifted me with the power of words
I help the scholar refine an important contribution in his field
The innocent young lady to impress a very special young man
A friend about to be fired to win a discrimination suit instead
The reckless young man to prove he should get his license back
The preacher to raise more money for his dream church building

Yet not a single word I write or speak or think or breathe or cry
breaks this loud and most deafening silence that separates me from
My Most Precious Love
So I pray using old, outdated, repetitive words-one bead at a time-
And from this archaic ritual I discover a new way to make love
to my King from far away and send a fleet of angels to guide his way.

Ross Conrad Galvan

SEPTEMBER 11

September 11 was a horrible event
Police were called and firemen sent
Thousands were killed while only some survived
Never to be forgotten, what a surprise!
Out of the ones that were killed two thirds were not found
Workers and volunteers have looked all around
Planes were hijacked to destroy this nation
They sought to create sheer devastation
We came together as a united power
To salute the lives lost in the Twin Towers.

Rune Leknes

A SILENT BLUBBER IN MY IGLOO

life is better when the lines are busy
those signals that you once had
flowing through your inner self
keeping it together as they stream
floating between the walls of denial
the distance you will get
above the thin air of illusions you craved
those signs of desperate needs
underneath the shell of emotional depth
you ride the distance without hearing the call
then life will be better as silence creeps in.

Ruth Daigon

NIGHT'S OTHER COUNTRY
A poem about making a settlement with death...
an acceptance of the inevitable.

>Before the great winds and the white noise
>of night, we'll cut loose from clocks and
>stand in fields spread out to nowhere singing mantras.
>
>Before the quiet waits in garments of goodbye,
>we'll bridge the silence of guitars
>and float sound to its center.
>
>Before hours burn to ash, we'll wrap ourselves
>in wind, in raw strips of light,
>our bodies wild as vines.
>
>Before land's end, we'll swim in all the rivers
>of the sky, and drown in sunlight,
>inhaling love as sweet as candlewick.
>
>Before our final season, let it be summer
>resonant with wings, vermouth of old sunrises,
>mountains growing slowly in the rain
>
>the light around us ripe and round
>and if it dies out, let it be extravagant,
>a marvel of darkness in night's other country.

Saaleha Bamjee

RANDOM THOUGHTS

Shatterings of crystal hope;
Shards of glassy thread,
Entwine their filaments around my heart
and weave their pattern in my head.

The broken dreams of long ago,
Now healed
but seem
more broken so.

Eluding illusions,
Unreal reality,
Shadows life and
Dampens ability.

Salvatore Amico M. Buttaci

THE GIFT HE GAVE

When God looked out at the world He made
And saw how His creatures had forgotten
His gift of creation,

When God saw the world rich in poverty,
Ruined by wars and filled with those
Empty of love,

And when God heard the hungry children
Crying, tricked, abandoned
In the streets,

When God thought of me, my brothers, sisters
Not yet born into that unsafe world,
He created our mother.

Santosh Kumar

THE POET & HOLY SPIRIT

I asked the Holy Spirit:
'Where's the ethos
That created Ten Commandments?
So many wars and now September eleven
Kashmir, Palestine burn and burn
Never in history such terrors perpetrated
Never before Satan so active
Chernobyl disaster, radiation poisoning
Anthrax poisoning
Is poison our destiny?
Bosnia, Somalia
Shameless ethnic bloodbath
Darkest period!'
Thus spoke the Holy Spirit:
'Buddhas, Prophets, Messiahs
Ever on the Cross
Always pray for mankind:
I've faith in Man
Only beware of fierce politicians
Marketing terrorists.
Hard lot!
Terrorism triumphed
As you went astray
Failed to listen to the soul's lark, your linnet
Failed to listen to Holy Ghost,
Guardian angels of inner self
And captains of your minds.'

Sean David Gregson

THE FOG

To roll upon the lushfull hills
a frolic fresh with melanchol'
a puffy dance of dew en-trance
in hardened land do drops a-fall.

Shield me from so brazen heat
mid-day rays cause swollen strife
creep and drip your spirit mass
pon' my mildly moistened life.

Dragons, snakes, and daffodils
clouds reform to give thee' sight
pressure paints a canvas new
strewn of colors soft and white.

Lay me pon' green mossy cliff
inundate with fog my face
flush away old mortal shell
Saturate with Grace this Place.

Sean Nugent

NATURE'S GIFT

The mountains grow but great oak trees in the distant sky
Clouds flow snow-white surrealistic waves upon the sunrise shores
Utter breathlessness of nature's breeze is nipping at a youthful waterfall
Whispering serenity orchestra of beauty painter of tranquillity
Sweeping across the rocks the fog settles calm thick warmth
A scenery of brush strokes flawless as a mothers faithful love
It's heaven sitting beyond the wings of the cities past the countryside's
Over the emerald hills and through the fields of dancing daffodils
Lays this beauty from a painter our Lord with soft tender strokes
A masterpiece of blissful art from him to me and you It's nature's gift.

CROSS OF LOVE

The pendulums swinging
And we just can't see the confusion in reality
Just a delusion fantasy in our minds
That love is real and sent from above
Not sent from a snake a lustful serpent beast
Who won't cease these emotions, fortified sinful sensations
Upon this cross of love

I've given my sacrifice
You've crucified my heart with your flaming lying eyes
Took my breath, took my soul, sent me straight to
agony from down below
Cut me open and let me bleed for love is nothing but a shame

Your lizard razor blade tongue is to blame
For ripping me apart and putting these nails in my hands
These rose thorns that dig so deep in my temples
Upon this cross of love

All hope is lost
As this spear cuts into my eyes and burns my tears
Cause there's too much confusion in a world of delusion
Was love sent from the heavens above by an angel dove
Or from down below ridding on a serpent of deception
It just doesn't seem right that these emotions blaze inside
They make me feel good; they make me feel bad
They make me glad; they make me sad
Upon this cross of love.

Serge van Duijnhoven

HOMEWARD BOUND

All strangers are born as children of their families
All strangers have played in houses they called home
On est tous des strangers. Travelers coming round
wandering through a space that everybody has to confiscate.
But where there's a will there's a way.
Stubbornness is what drives us all and drives us crazy.
To live fully from the land the soil in which the seeds are
spread with the hand.
The hair on our heads is as the cane on our roofs.
Our cracked skin is as the eroded walls of our shags.
Transparency is the scare of our bones.
Our voice cries at best for help.
What we are seeking is rest.
Asylum in eternity.
What we are is where we have been
falling: cerebral hunters and hunted prey.
We are game in the woods. A hungry flock in nature's
hungry mouth. We are obedient and futile.
Tiny particles floating around. Our names have been assigned
and even the gift of life was not our choice.
Every single good we own and everything we are
is borrowed, shareware, bonds and loans. Property
of Time alone; that vicious, greedy stockbroker
and billionaire, who having been born without a soul
supports no other soul as company. Who has no friends
or relatives, and rules the earth as if he were the master of the universe.

We owe him all - as he insists - and everybody has to pay
His will is merciless. No exceptions, no delays.
Who prays for help, will be harassed.
Who disobeys, will disappear. He holds us hostage
Nobody is free to stay. We have to leave and sneak out like thieves.
When evening comes we pack our bags.
We cross the border in the thick of night.
Our exitpapers are called: death.

Shabnam Abdoola

SILENCE

A tear slips silently
down a tender cheek
A fair hand trembles
Quickly waving it away
Why are we silenced by Violence
Why are we shy to cry
Sorrow rips us apart
Yet our mouths are clamped shut
Our hearts filled with horror
Our faces remain icy and hard
why are we silenced
by the shocking violence
around us each day
against which we even fear to Pray
The tell-tale look of horror
The cries nobody hears
These broken mirrors
Reflect our shattered souls
A sign that we are
Living flesh & flowing blood
Not scaly skin & transparent
Shatterproof Glass.

Shalini Nayar

IS THIS LOVE?

Is this love
the crashing waves of scattered memories
that laughs and giggles along with my schoolgirl silliness
only to be choked by reality?

is this love
when every minute smells of you
even as I try to immobilize my senses
my heart flutters helplessly like a caged butterfly,
that is wingless and beautiful?

is this love
the aftertaste of bitterness
that lives on the edges of unpleasant dreams
when I couldn't feel the way I used to feel?

so is this love then
a tapestry of escapism only our feelings can weave?

Sharon W. Flynn

FOREVER CHANGING MOON

Upwards towards a changing Moon,
lifetimes reaching the stars within...
I found love in the forever you.

Forever...climbing starry steps
to reach beyond the earthly pull
of love with beginnings
and endings. To lift
the soul to a higher plane
where a matching soul waits...
too be united, to plunge into
the mysteries of the deep, the eternal.

I hear the continuous echo
of your heartbeat calling to me.
And, I know I am not alone
in this universe. I am wrapped
in the upwards flow of a changing
Moon, lifetimes reaching the stars
within my soul. Forever love
never-ending, ever building

~~~~~eons upon eons.

SPIRIT FLUTE UNENDING

My Sweet One,
hear the sultry strains
of my spirit flute...

mellow notes floating
on sound waves
right into your heart.
My love is a new melody
sung with unending yearning.

O', Fair One, I play
the notes of your soul. They
are yours to hold onto forever.
Yet, forever is too short,
infinity not long enough.
My spirit flute will breathe
the same song unending.
It will be an unseen hand
to caress your yearning spirit,
an eternal arm to rest upon
the shoulder of your need.

Listen to the sensuous strains
of the spirit flute, My Love.
They are carried upon the notes
of my own heart, my own soul.

Shawnte Orion

DREAMS (N.)
—first published in The Peralta Press

    mysterious river
    connecting
    lake and sea

    you lie on an embankment
    eyes closed, plunging
    hand into stream
    grasping at powerful currents
    water flowing between your fingers
    rushing toward the sea

    you stand
    empty handed
    but notice your hand still wet
    water dripping from each finger
    as the Sun dries your arm.

Sherri Anderson

HIDDEN DESTINY

There are some connections that defy time and space.
Stronger than anything either of us have experienced.
These feelings must remain hidden, never revealed,
But their fires burn stronger in their silence.
Maybe you will never know the depth of my love for you
I can't explain the way I feel,
I only know that I can't help it.
Unexpectedly, you stole my heart.
Was this love sparked by chance?
What coincidence brought us together?
Such harmony has never existed between two
You seem to know me as no other.
I no longer question it, or fight it.
It's as if our spirits have always been joined
Two souls waiting for their time to be together
A destiny that we discovered one day,
When we realized the bond between us.
It defies reason and circumstance,
Maybe it can be denied for a time...
But it will never be stopped.

Sheryl Mackiernan

FOREVER LOYAL

What is family
The men and women who shared the way they look
their strange talents, even stranger flaws
They shared everything except the most vital
love, time, cradle of support

Understanding this is teaching the earth why it circles the sun
lost family orbits through the mind everyday
of every endless year
until its sun blinds the eyes with its mystery

Could it be so simple to comphrend
My loyalty is undying until the end.

Shirley Bolstok

THE REALITY OF NUMBER EIGHT

The skies are turning gray and the rivers are running
The rain will soon be thundering upon the plains
I see his soul over the horizon, so close, so far away
The deluge will drown his semblance in refrain
Others, but not like him, have loved me
Only he has been favored for his pain
Seven men have proceeded him
Seven men have become his game
My guise is the timekeeper upon his wall
Seven kinsmen have caused his wait
Our karma is the hand of time
He is the reality of number eight
Seven times I have walked this path
Now it is me who must compensate
I must be punished for his redemption
It is the requirement of number eight
The rains wallow in weeping grass
The birds fly in circles in search of food
There is war beneath the waters
Where the earth quakes and rivers brood
There are footsteps where he searches for me
Spinning specters out of angel hair
He remains among the shadows
Sleeping upon the lions lair
Seven men have walked before him
Their memories thrown upon the sod

For only he can join my side
My nemesis chosen by God
I tarry silently beneath my slumber
Till he is finished hunting for my soul
For my counterpart to become my half
I must hold my heart to remain whole
Seven strongholds have brought him here
I behold now, the trepidation of my fate
He has conquered seven hearts before me
He is the reality of number eight.

FIELDS OF WILD INDIGO

I beheld you and a transformation occurred
I saw your heart in a fledgling bird
Your eyes reflected amber lights of the horizon
Mysterious and twinkling like the golden sun
I remembered dreams that had long gone by
Fading into the vapor of an ambiguous sky
You were holding them in the palm of your hand
Rebuilding into angels out of drifting sand
You were magical, unyielding, seeing through
Not of the world, for the world was of you
Even when I hated you, birds sang your song
Reminding of the enchantment that made me strong
Your smile created the sunshine and gentle breeze
Your moods created thunderstorms and raging seas
Brooding passions hurled into a turbulent swell
Your cries and laughter caught in the rain that fell
How could I forget when everything I breathe is you
When I look ahead I'm always seeing through
I discern your whisper calling in the wind
Not knowing where it ends, or where you begin
You live in every shape and form of my heart

When I walk the earth we are never apart
Your spirit dances in fields of wild indigo
Your soul's colors in spectrums of the rainbow
Untamed and exquisite, changing in brilliant cast
And when I transcend this life, looking into my past
Lingering, wondering, what the afterlife will bring
I'll gaze into my life knowing I have seen everything
You were the colors of love ever-changing in hue
I will have seen the world, for I saw everything in you.

Shivendra N Green

SUCCESS

The path of success is a maze
Not seen through the gloomy haze
of twisted one-sided ways,
but in fact there is more than one "right-track."
Or pathway to the map of the trail
overcoming challenges entails
the fighting courage to prevail
in the midst of this hell
planning to succeed and never to fail
keep on going, break the barrier scale
Have faith and it'll turn out well...

Sonia Edwards

RIGHT NOW

As we sat and talked,
I saw the way you looked at me.
The way your eyes called for me,
And how your touch told me everything.
I saw that you wanted to hold me.
I, too, wanted to be in your arms.
Can you read my eyes?
They are saying that it's ok.
That one day we will have each other.
Right now, though, is not the time.
But I heard it, I felt it,
When you said "I Love You"
I know it would be ok.

Stanislaus Jaworski

BIRD'S LAMENT

The nest she made of twigs
and leafs suitable to his
taste and her beak
the feathers and kapok
for the inside, soft and warm.

The storm made an end
to it all, her neck broken
the eggs turned to broken shells
He was hopping up and down
along the ruins of life.

Steve Murray

SO BE IT

aliens come from outer space,
come to change the human race,
spray 'em all with tins of mace,
human technology, we're off the pace,
what a waste, a total disgrace.

alien crafts arrive in packs,
their space suits are totally black,
their alien names printed on their backs,
you can't fault these, their are no cracks,
torture 'em, quick get the racks,
that'll send 'em back!

off they go with a flash of light,
i have to say i got a fright,
sent 'em home with great delight,
thinking back they were quite polite,
will they come back well they might.

Steven Valentine

PHOENIX

From the dieing embers
Leaps a spark
Flames rekindle
Glow and dwindle.

The fire takes flight
And flame becomes feather
A gleaming beak
Pushes through coals reborn.

Phoenix rising
Higher than high
Flaming feathers
Take to the sky.

A bird, once molten
Solidified
Such smouldering beauty
Redefined.

Stuart Jason Deutsch

OUR JOURNEY

From friends, to lovers, to soulmates
were standing side by side.
To conjure up the faith that ties the knot,
and unifies our lives.
As we get ready for the epic battle ahead,
our mission on Earth is clear.
We shall sail on together, defeat every fear.
Amidst the shadows of doubt, and anxiety in the mind.
We will be fine if one doesn't leave the other behind.

Troubled times are sure to come.
Communication a priority, to difficult for some.
In time it will be clear to all
that we were meant to be.
We will sit side by side beneath the willow tree.
Then as we wake to morning sun,
we will know the battle is won.
For you are all I need,
stay with me now and forever,
I love you...indeed!

Sudheesh V Nair

RAINDROPS

When the rain stops and the sun shines again
I will start looking for my color in the sky
It never occurs to me as how clear my vision was
when my mind was not as fouled as it is now

Then, sitting on the window sill stretching my arms
through the grill to touch the dripping drop of rain
everything astonied me, like, the bird that sat on the
branch dousing, but ostensibly not minding

The feeling of cold rain drops touching my palm
always used to change form in to the luring need to
run out and play in the stream that flows
right in front of my home, just for me ..

Now, standing here, impatiently waiting for the
"darned" rain to stop so I can continue my
endless race towards my vacuous goals
It is a sham to even think back and take a deep breath!

Susan K. Rowse

DIXIE WALTZ

She recalls the silly, insidious jerk
The nuance of pleasure of a mysterious quirk
From eyes that penetrate from across the room
Smiles half-mooned with a passionate zoom
Hair all a mess with blonde springing curls
Draping around eyes of this sensitive girl
Pulled to the sight of a man in a shadow
All lobed up with his mane in an ebb flow
Looks like a wolf...perish the thought
"Me, am I Goldilocks?" Dressed out and fraught!
Knees shake to rattle...tremors to nerves
Eyes bold and frightened...dancing on curves
Hands reach...extend...floating the swirl
Taffeta cinched on the bust of this girl
Presenting the orbs of porcelain globes
Seduced eyes of shadows beginning their probe
Floats of two bodies graceful through crowds
Clutching hands weaving as forms take a bow
This beauty to all and stranger to some
Take up this waltz as rumors from tongues
Chatter the beat as pulses festoon
The character of dance and this free flowing room
These two ever friends swirl smiles with their feet
Swinging and turning to a waltz made of heat
Stars seem to drift on fragrant bouquets
For dances with Belles and Rebels with ways
The hoop skirts of lace and taffeta bows

Jasmine in hair that gently repose
The gray of a uniform worn by this Johnny
The eyes of his lady...his bonnie blue Bonnie
He takes in her smile...her nose like a pixie
The waltzes of yesterday...bygones of Dixie.

Susie Davies

DAD

If I could wish upon a star and make my dreams come true
I'd wish for immortality and most of all for you
If I knew that I would lose you I would have begged for you to stay
I know it would have made no difference as you had to go away
I think of you a lot now, have your pictures everywhere
Most of all I think of you when I hold my Mother near.

Taylor Graham

FATHER AT 87

A child, I stretched my legs to match
his stride, short-shanked Pennsylvania stock.
The only way to get there was patiently,
on foot, no questions. Save your breath,
it's a good two miles to the waterfall.

He always reached the vista far ahead
of me. And then the long hike back,
sidetracking for whatever secrets
the woods held: a rusting beaver trap,
what's left of an old hewn cabin;
wisteria grown wild. Frogs by a pond,
buckskins in a meadow.

I've followed him, short-shanked,
too eager for the vista-end
of trails. He's so far ahead
now, he can't even tell me
what the view is.

Thelma Shutters

ANGEL OF DEATH

    I do not fear the angel of death
    For he will be sent from the best
    To take me home to his great land
    This angel he sends to hold our hand
    So I won't have to go home alone
    To sit with him upon his throne
    The Angel of Death will be my light
    He'll take me on a glorious flight
    GODS love and comfort he will bring
    As I go home his angels will sing
    A wondrous flight I have in store
    When the Angel of Death comes to my door
    A lot of people his presence they fear
    To me I'll know my LORD is near
    To take me away from pain and strife
    No more I'll suffer in this life
    All crippled up I'll be no more
    I'll stand straight to meet the LORD
    I will walk upon streets of gold
    When I get there I'll never grow old
    So the Angel of Death do not fear
    He only comes when our LORD is near.

Thomas Fortenberry

BOMBAY

    Bombay is impossibly packed:
    Sardines, a can of humanity
    Broken open before the world;
    Ancient, fragrant, alive,
    Squirming, wriggling through the mud,
    Blowing out the candles on the beaches,
    Elephanta Island afloat in the harbor;
    The sun now touching the horizon
    Both dusk and dawn in one hazy moment
    On the birthday festival Ganesh Chaturthi,
    Just another day in the life of the elephant-faced,
    Four-armed, good luck with twenty fingers crossed
    With all the little fishes swimming circles
    Between dangling toes in recurrent tides.

Timothy McNeal

ALL SOULS DAY

Lovely ladies,
like
of old,
clutching at umbrellas
like
troopers at their parachutes,
with looks
like
weeping windscreen wipers.

Tina K Campbell

THE FACTS OF LIFE

Russian temptress
I was weak.
Away with the soul so shy and meek.
Lost in a sombrero haze
Woke up cold
Had better days
Rainbow high with taste sublime
Water Melon, Peach, Pineapple
Lime!
Conversations, laughter fills the air
Difference is that I'm not there
You however stay the same
Never mind the hate or shame
It's a fact of life
Who said it was fair?
Tell it to him
He's no longer there.

Todd Burge

UP IN THE WEST VIRGINIA HILLS

Man I'm tired of all the driving
And the ringin' in my ears
Tired of all the balding tires
And feeling older than my years
I'd trade it all in this minute
Place the brakes upon the thrills
For a quiet life without the heartaches
Up in the West Virginia hills

See I wore out that old Geo
And now I wear this way I feel
I feel my fingers bleeding
While needing
Something old and weak to kill
You see these strings they just don't love me
I know now that they never will
My love is waiting
She's tucked away
Up in those West Virginia hills

I got a brother in Wood County
Says he'll help keep me on my feet
Change in my head and in my pockets
A place to bed a place to eat
You see my ink
It stopped flowing

I got the lead out
And it stayed still
I need a life with fewer verses
I need the West Virginia hills

So pour me a drink while the moon shines
And we'll laugh and talk about our old times
Take these keys
They're no longer mine
And tell my mother I'm finally fine
Take the six-string dream and let it go
To the bottom of the Ohio
Let the muddy water fill up the sound hole
Down down down it'll go
I need a life without these heartaches
My sick heart doesn't need a pill
It needs the hills of WV
It needs the WV hills.

Tony Bush

NINETEEN STARS

In half-vacant streets bowl entangled rag and bone
Of the memories rising to greet the day,
Then sinking again when twilight clamps jaws
That chew and consume the light away.

On perimeter fences, tattered and torn
Hang sadly the keepsakes of words and toys;
When the rain melts the words and moths eat the cloth
What remains for the nineteen girls and boys?

How violently taken, snatched and snuffed,
Poor candles blown out in a hurricane blast;
Their innocent lives of all possible futures,
Had barely begun, then suddenly passed.

What keepers of reason could ever explain
To the faces of children that wonder and weep,
Any semblance of logic why ones such as they
Were erased in an instant, banished to sleep?

It is kinder to speak of the nineteen stars
Born of nineteen souls passing into the night
And their angelic eyes shining down with a gleam,
Shining down from the heavens, eternal and bright.

Tony Weaver

AT LAST

Daylight slides
Into the night
Using up oxygen
While taking away
All sight.
Dusk must settle
Before the coming
Of dawn.
Life is twisting and turning
But must go on.
Sadness blurs
Into joy.
Lies are mixed
With the truth
In an endless ploy.
In the darkest - deepest
crevices of our mind
We search and learn
As the light continues
To shine.
This eternal glow
Represents our existence
Simply by trusting in it
Suddenly - we come
To know.
Hidden meanings

Discovered truths
Believable possibilities
All present from
Birth.
Lightening flashes
Across the sky
Finally- we can go forward
At last - knowing why.

Torey Fraley

ORCHID LEAVES

    Mirror to the shape, the vision
of a petal's grace, we radiate,
a paradox in silence;
old & young, men & women
mounted on the single stem
of a few well chosen words.

    Growing together, thoughts
like water to the parched soil of our minds,
we few become a garden,
blossoms tenderly evoked
from these least promising of seeds.

Troels Hundtofte

MURDER VS MURDER

Cause I die.
When you're romancing your bombs
And I cry.
When you cherish martyrs.
And every child that is abused
by principles, and hate.
Everyone is loosing ground
to anger and revenge.

Now tell me, what did you see in his eyes?
When you blew him away?
What did you see? was he killer,
or just a child?

A child lies broken on the ground.
not quite dead but unconscious.
there's a lie inside of us
We are conserving wounds.

In the dawn of
senseless slaughter
We instigate
killers as saviors.

This is murder vs. murder
This is death vs. death
This murder vs. murder
This blood vs. blood.

Uppalapati Lakshmi Prasanthi

TO HUSBANDS ALL OVER THE WORLD

("You" means representative for Husbands.
"She" is a representative for Wives.)

You want her to be beautiful
Do you ever notice?
The beauty of a woman when she feels shy
while you are looking at her with love
The beauty of a woman when she is
thinking of you in solitude

You want her to be healthy
Do you ever notice?
The sense of strength in a woman
when she is surrounded by you
The spirit of work in her even she is ill
when she is in your company

You want her to be happy
Do you ever notice?
The feeling of joy and gay
when she walks in hand with you along the way
the sense of pride and merry
to hear all that you say, to share your heart

When can you know?
A woman feels you as her real wealth
you are the source of her happiness and health
It is your love, rather than the sense of duty
that make her the real beauty.

Venessa Aquilla Hall

CHAINED MIND DETAINED

Clicked instances when the world ceases to exist and the times begin;
Who states what's crazy in your mind and how they think it works;
I don't know your thoughts and why should I?
I believe I have much better things to do;
At least important than to know your mind;
You've seen movies of chained up beast who go wild with
uncontrolled movement' who says we are not all like that?
Chained to our mind and obligations
like a tight choker around our thoughts.
I'd like to believe that the world is all good but
I know its not but I don't have to rub my nose in the filth around me.
I refuse to be week and detained;
I learn from the mistakes around me;
I do not think I am better than most,
There are others better than me the simple fact is don't
be degraded by others are wallow in there filth,
stick your head out like a bird and soar away on the good.

W. S. Mayo

TWO SIDES
(for John)

     He never knew which side of the tracks to stand on.
     On one side were the shiny shoes and bell-bottomed
     pants of the dilettantes who had been his patrons;
     on the other were the alcoholics and
     skid row bums of which he felt a certain romance.
     It was a game of wandering turned over to solitaire and
     then to Russian roulette.
     And when the train bore down on him his last thought
     was that he was simply sorry he had never said hello.

Ward Kelley

HIS SINGULAR INITIAL

A single poem, bred well,
will race far ahead of all

the other thoughts in a poet's
mind, for most thoughts are

laden with the cares of our
existence: how to drag these

bones from place to place
while providing them an

adequate nourishment. But
a poem has no such baggage,

and instead gallops through
the brain, never in circles, but

always straight to the finish
line where it rises on two legs,

screaming a horse's thin exclamation
and only then do you see the black-

caped rider who unveils his arm
to slash his wicked sword at your

naked chest then rides off, leaving
you marked with his singular initial.

Artist's Note:
Galileo (1564-1642), in his "The Assayer" wrote, "I say that the testimony of many has little more value than that of few, since the number of people who reason well in complicated matters is much smaller than that of those who reason badly. If reasoning were like hauling I should agree that several reasoners would be worth more than one, just as several horses can haul more sacks of grain than one can. But reasoning is like racing and not like hauling, and a single Barbary steed can outrun a hundred dray horses."

William Dean Hamilton

TIME

If time heals all wounds,
Then why aren't mine?
My blood has boiled away,
Turned to dust.
I see over a thousand miles or years,
But not my backyard.
The rose that was supposed to bloom,
Is now a vine around my neck.
If time heals all wounds,
Then why aren't mine?

William James Jenkinson

EMOTIONAL ROLLERCOASTER

Sitting with my head against a void of blue sky.
You're not to blame.
First date in vivid colour, clear as summer
You reached to meet my hand halfway.
Took possession of my heart.
Began my ride on the emotional
Roller-coaster.
Elation, despair.

Looking over my shoulder as I round each corner
Treading forward hoping to find the past, a fleeting moment lost in a wave of sorrow.
Aware of the embers that still glow, smoulder.
You are there at the moment of awareness,
Before eyes see the light of morning.
Travel the route of day until sleep brings respite.
Frustration of a love unrequited.

NOBODYS' LOVE

Nobody really cares for you,
Yet someone shares your nights
And nobody wants to hold you
Until morning spreads its light
Nobody loved you before and
Nobody loves you more
Than someone.

Nobody hides the feelings that
Someone is allowed to show
And someone gets to take you
Where nobody wants to go
Someone is all that he can be
And someone holds the envy
Of nobody.

Yvonne Sparkes

THE ROBIN

A blush of red adorns your coat
Oh maestro of the warbled note.
In song you stand at heaven's door,
Those warbled songs that you implore
How can a hardened heart remain,
Without a falling tear to claim?
Through weather's good or bad you sing,
Remind the listener of spring.
Perhaps to give a faith of kind,
That summer is not far behind.
So sing my little feathered friend
Hope and joy in song you lend.
Faith and trust that come what may,
There will always be a brighter day.

NOTES ON CONTRIBUTORS

Adam Wang: Poet from Colorado, USA.

Agnes Cowan from Georgia, USA believes: "Poetry is meant to be shared, since anything is only half of what it is intended to be if unshared."

Alberto O Cappas from NY, USA is a graduate of the State University of NY. He is also the author of "*Disintegration of the Puerto Ricans*", a collection of poems, published in 1997.

Alice Pero is from CA, USA; a dancer, musician and poet/teacher; widely published in many magazines and anthologies; her first book of poetry, *Thawed Stars*, illustrated by Bruce Silton, published in 1999; awarded by The National League of American Pen Women. Alice has taught creative writing on both U.S. coasts and was a creative writing workshop leader for the New York City Ballet Education Department's poetry project from 1991 through 1996, teaching in inner city school of the five boroughs of New York as well as being poet-in-residence at a private school in New Jersey.

Alisha Nicole Hubbard from Oregon, USA says: "I started writing poetry when I was 14....poetry is an opportunity to express one's feelings about a subject.... the best written poetry comes from the heart, or when it is written with such feeling that you cant help but want to read or hear more."

Amos Taiwo: Well-known poet from Lagos, Nigeria; author of immortal poem "The Ancient Warrior"; published in the June 2002 Issue of *Taj Mahal Review*.

Andrea Venantius: Poet from Ontario, Canada; her family originally being from parts of India and Pakistan; published in several literary magazines and anthologies.

Andrena Zawinski from CA, USA is Feature Editor at PoetryMagazine.com and San Francisco Bay Area Poets for Peace co-chair. She is a teacher of college writing and freelance literary assistant. Her full collection, *Traveling in Reflected Light*, was released by Pig Iron Press as a Kenneth Patchen poetry competition winner. Her latest chapbook is from Pudding House Publications, *Andrena Zawinski's Greatest Hits 1991-2001.*

Andrew from Nottinghamshire, England is an amateur poet "I try to write mainly from my own experiences, feelings and emotions."

Andy Harding from Plymouth, United Kingdom says: " I'm 40 years old, write poetry in my spare time. Currently divorced but have a partner, with two children from previous marriage. Poetry is my hobby, not my profession."

Angeli'ca J. Varney: Poet from Ohio, USA.

Ani Gjika was born in Tirane, Albania; now resides in Massachusetts; published in *3rd Muse Poetry Journal, Stirring, MiPo, Melic Review, NakedPoetry*, and others.

Anita Barrows from California, USA is a poet, translator, essayist and clinical psychologist. A recipient of many awards, including an NEA grant for Poetry, she recently co-translated Rilke's Book of Hours with Joanna Macy. Anita lives and works in Berkeley, California. She happily divides her time between her psychology practice, her commitment to writing and, most importantly, her devotion to her two daughters and granddaughter.

Annastasiya Alexandra from New York, USA wrote: "A poem can only be as fruitful as its creator. I believe my poetry whispers my life.... Thoughts, feelings, wants, wishes, sorrows, pleasures, and secrets are hidden within each and every line."

Annette Stone from TN, USA is married homemaker with two children. The poet writes "poetry for inner peace."

Annie Finch from OH, USA is Associate Professor of creative writing at Miami University. Her books of poetry include *EVE* (Story Line Press, 1997). Her new book *CALENDARS* will be published by Tupelo Press in early 2003 and her translation of the complete poetry of Louise Labe will be published soon by University of Chicago Press. She has also published a critical book on poetics and edited several anthologies on poetry.

Arthur E. Holland Sr lives in Illinois, USA; poet, creative writer, fiction, parody, non-fiction wordsmith performer; physically challenged. (wheelchair bound) educator, television producer (CAN-TV). "I am a beautiful black creature, articulate and intelligent but not egoistic, married 38 yrs. two college educated sons. And a true lover of life."

Audrey A Cooper is from CA, USA. She says, "I am a published Therapeutic Poetry Writer. Also, I am a mother, wife, marriage and children consultant for 40 years, helping women cope with relationships and life experiences, bringing their feelings, thoughts, and emotions on Romance, Love, Relationships, Marriage, Men, Children, Religion, through my poetry. It makes me happy if someone can identify or see a message in the words I write!"

Dr Ayo Millers from is a lecturer of history and coordinator of population census at the University of Ilorin Nigeria.

Ayumi "Goldie" Kato from Odawara-shi, Japan writes haiku, poems and Japanese short stories on the Internet.

Balog Anna: Poet from Gothenburg, Sweden.

Barbara Hardcastle from Texas, USA wrote: "I am married and a homemaker. I have lived in Pleasanton, Texas for 33 years. I have been writing poetry for three years now. I love to express words on paper that exhibits feeling and compassion." Her poems have appeared in *The Fabric of A Vision* and *Taj Mahal Review.*

Beatrice O'Brien from NY, USA sends the following bio: "Navy Nurse WWII, Author of a non-fiction narrative, *ONE TRACK*, A collection of journal entries, *LOON LAKE JOURNAL*, editor, Poetry Reading Series Director (20 yrs.) And workshop leader. Mother of 6, married for 57 yrs. Volunteer in a creative writing project for veterans."

Bertha Rose Young from Georgia, USA says: "I am a wife and mother of five children and two boy chi; Mexican dogs; they think I am mama too; all children are grown and all the grandchildren are but one girl 5 years old;; paw and my pride and joy; one dog is fat[baby[the other slim and trim [Smokey] this story is about them."

Beth Grindstaff from TN, USA says: " I am a 21 year old college student majoring in radiologic technology. I have been writing since I was 12, and have had poetry published in several different publications."

Betty Hapgood from E Sussex, Britain sends the following biography: "Betty Hapgood has spontaneous combustion in her hat, because she is decrepit. Mystic pillows say "Boo!" Betty Hapgood is the nude motorcycle beauty at midnight. She is Nirvana's granny."

Birdie from Texas, USA is a poet and shortstory writer; interested in singing and songwriting, painting, drawing, sketching art work; has been an extra in a movie. "This Texas lady enjoys busying herself writing many types of poetry haiku, rhyme, non-rhyme, inspirational, humor, dark and therapeutic."

Bitte Assarmo from Bandhagen, Sweden is a freelancing writer. She writes poems, short stories and also works at an internet site called Labyrinth, writing book and film reviews. The poet lives with her husband, a thirteen-year-old son and her dog in Stockholm.

Bogdan Tiganov from London, UK is a Romanian born writer with a vision. He has written and published three books: one book is poetry, called *11 Year Old Refugee*, the other two are experimental fantasy, called *Fakery and Tarnish*.

Brandon Miracle: Poet from NC, USA.

Brazos N. Mason was born in Texas, USA; lives in Houston; truck driver; interested in golf, poetry, short stories [in that order]; his immortal poem "Darkness" appeared in *The Still Horizon*.

Brent M. Parker: Poet from CA, USA; currently working on a fantasy novel set in modern New York and a musical play about how rebellion has changed between the 60's and today.

Carlos Hiraldo from NY, USA sends the following bio: "I'm 30 years old and currently an English Professor at LaGuardia Community College in Queens, New York. While receiving my Ph.D. in English Literature from Stony Brook University, I was co-editor for four years of the school literary magazine, *Snark: A Journal of Poetry & Translations*."

Camilla E Clark: Poet from East Sussex, England.

Chanda Witherspoon is from GA, USA. She was born in Miami FL. The poet says, "I have always been a free spirited person. I have been writing poetry for over 10 years. I began writing poetry because it was a way for me to express my inner being. Within writing I am allowed to be creative, to be free. I reach others through my words. Poetry has always been a great passion of mine. Writing is another form of who I am, like listening to jazz and dancing to music that allows me to be free. I enjoy this gift."

Dr. Charles Albano from New Jersey, USA is an Adjunct Professor of Management at Fairleigh Dickinson University in America. He published a widely-circulated book entitled *Transactional Analysis on the Job through the American Management Association*. He has written numerous articles on management and interpersonal relations that appear in print and on the Internet. He has been writing poetry for over ten years and recently completed five books of poetry available at Booksurge.com

Charlotte Peters Rock; Poet from Cheshire, England.

Chelsea Comeau: Poet from British Columbia, Canada.

Chiesa Irwin lives in the tropical part of Queensland in northern Australia. Main concerns are for the safety and well being of the planet and all its people and animals. The poem "OCHRE" is in honour of the rural women who work on the land.

Christine A Kempster from Herts, Great Britain told Cyberwit: "I turned 50 with the millennium, and with the changes to the century came my own personal changes, I began to put words down on paper, I went back to school, learning to teach. Now I am me, not merely wife, mother, sister or daughter, but me!"

Christopher R. Akins supplied the following bio: "Just your average fella living his average life, doing average things to make himself happy.... I live in Tampa, Florida, currently involved with self, not to be confused with being self absorbed, which is a waste of energies, in my opinion. I am a part of www.queerpoets.com....currently writing a manuscript, for a play, and doing some commercial illustrations for a newspaper here... "

Corrine De Winter: Poet from Mass, USA.

Cynthia Therese Hoffman from MN, USA says: " I have been writing poetry for 26 years, and I have just recently started sharing my gift with the world. An avid gardener, dreamer and someone who takes the time to enjoy the true beauty that life and nature have to offer. Writing poetry is my escape and true love. It takes me to beautiful places I've always dreamed I would someday visit." Her extraordinary poem "Nature's Enchantment!" appeared in *The Still Horizon*.

Damon D. Brewer: Poet from AR, USA.

Dande Lampa Matusalem: Poet from CA, USA.

Daniel William Gonzales from CA, USA is a 24-year college student in Whittier, California at Cal State Fullerton. He is studying for a degree in English Literature/Journalism. His poems were published in *The Fabric of A Vision* and *The Still Horizon*.

Darius Gabriel Bugarin, born in Nueva Ecija, Philippines, son of Pablo and Evelyn Bugarin is a published poet under poetry.com.

Dave Slater: Poet from Cumbria, UK.

David Hill (b. 1971) lives in Budapest, Hungary; published two collections, Angels and Astronauts and Bald Ambition. His free quarterly leaflet *LYRIKLIFE* features examples of his published work, including translations from German, Hungarian, Romanian and Russian. Visit the poet at www.lyriklife.com.

Deanna Dale Horton is fifth generation northern Californian and 3/4 Southern. Horton attended University at California State University, Chico, where she received her BA in political science, then furthered her education in literature and writing at Georgia State University in Atlanta. Currently Horton resides in Sacramento, CA with her partner Shan, and a close proximity to her family.

Dr. Deborah FerBer: Born in Frieberg Germany and moved to USA; a successful Entrepreneur, Business Manager, and Counselor; several undergraduate and graduate degrees in Art, Sociology, Management, Psychology and Doctorate in Business Administration. When asked, "What do you do" Dr. Deborah FerBer usually replies that she is a "philosopher of life" and explains that what she likes to do is think and observe people and events.

Deborah J. Norris from Ohio, USA provided: "I am a housewife and mother of 3 children. I have a 23-year-old daughter, and 17-year-old son, and had a son that was 8 when he passed away. I just started writing poems about 4 or 5 months ago... My thoughts and innermost feelings come out through my writings."

Deborah Russell from Maryland, USA shared the following biography: "Sec, International Art Galleries Assoc 86-90, MD Congress-PTA, 89-91,KIDZART! 85-98. VP-Ex Bd, Art Institute & Gallery 91-98. Owner/Manager: Parallels Studio & Gallery 95-98.Workshops: Delaware DSS, United Way & SCA 94-96 Exhibits: Artists Market, Cultural Diversity, SSU 94-98. Solo exhibits: Parallels, Public Libraries of Sussex & Kent Counties in Delaware, Wicomico & Worcester Counties of Maryland. Member: National Writer's Union - East, The Poetry Society of America; NYC, World Haiku Club, Founder: Susumu Takaguchi, The Maryland Poetry & Literary Society, Baltimore Writers Alliance, The Poetry Project, NYC and Life Member of The World Academy Arts & Culture/World Congress Poets."

Debra Marie Reilly: Poet from CA, USA.

Del Senkbeil from Wisconsin, USA is a retired secretary with 500 poems copyrighted on different websites. "Many of my poems are sensual love poems."

Dianne M. Sherwin: Poet from WI, USA.

Dustin: Poet from PA, USA.

Ed Zipek: Poet from NJ, USA.

Edith A. Jenkins from CA, USA was born in San Francisco October 12, 1916. Her published books are the following: *Divisions on a Ground*, Lapis Press, Santa Monica, 1986. *Against a Field Sinister*, City Lights Books, San Francisco, 1991. *The Width of a Vibrato*, Pennywhistle Press, Sante Fe, 1990. *Selected Poems*, Black Star Press, San Francisco, 2001.

Elisha Porat: Poet from Ein Hahoresh, Israel.

Prof. Elsy Satheesan lives in Virginia, USA; has been teaching English and American literature at graduate and post graduate levels for nearly 30 yrs in Kerala, India; published nationally, internationally and in USA, in different anthologies.

Emma Burgin: Poet from NC, USA.

Elvira Selow: Poet from Bad Nauheim, Germany.

Eve Hall is from Ohio, USA; an African American published writer and poet; won several writing contests; published in several zines, including, *"Skyline Publications" "Mature Living"* and *"Rainy Day Corners."* "Some of my goals are to publish my poetry manuscripts and my children's books."

F. William Broome from GA, USA says: "My home in the Blue Ridge Mountains provides much of my resources for poetry. However, memories and contrasts during earlier years, must be written about. Some of my work is published in the United States and other countries."

Filipe Miguel Gomes: Poet from Florida, USA.

Francis Figueroa: Poet from Florida, USA.

Frank Anthony Ph.D. is from Vermont, USA; President of New England Writers; author of poetry, essays and interviews published in literary journals, magazines and newspapers of the United States, England and Canada. He and his wife are the Directors of the NEW contests, annual conference and anthology now in their 14th year. He has created a new poetry form, the BRIK,

22 spaces/characters wide which in Courier new font is a perfect rectangle. His BRIK poems have appeared in Canada, England, India and the US. His beautiful poem "Jewish Unlucky Numbers" was published in *Taj Mahal Review*.

Fred Marmorstein from VA, USA says: "I have been fortunate enough to publish fiction in *Salt River Review* and *Moonwort Review*, and *Joe*. And, I have recently been featured on *Poetry SuperHighway*. I teach Language Arts in an alternative high school in Manassas, Virginia."

Gary Lehmann is from New York, USA; teaches short story writing and poetry at Writers & Books in Rochester, NY, the Rochester Instute of Technology, and has been the Writer in Residence at Roberts Wesleyan College; poetry and short stories widely published — about 60 pieces a year; the director of the Athenaeum Poetry group. See www.creekwalker.com.

Geraldine Sarmiento: Poet from MI, Italy.

Geertruud Ida Maria: Poet from Zwolle, Netherlands; a freelance copywriter for the local papers and an art painter. Her excellent poem "Butterfly" was published in International Journal *Taj Mahal Review*.

Ginny Christiansen from NSW, Australia is "33 year old mother of 4 who has just rekindled her love of writing."

Giovanni Ghirga MD: Poet from Rome, Italy; published in *The Still Horizon* and *Taj Mahal Review*. "I am a Pediatrician and after having been cared for ill children for more than 20 years I have developed a sense of incomprehension for our society. Puppies of lions play before to be able to hunt. Many children cannot play because must work!"

Goldie Mae from Western Australia says: "I believe it was Lord Byron said all I wish to say: But words are things, and a small drop of ink, /Falling, like dew, upon a thought, produces /That which makes thousands, perhaps millions, think."

Gregory W Bryant was born in Atlantic City, NJ but now resides in Greensboro, NC with his son. His published book of poetry is *"Poems of the Heart VOL. II"*

Harold Janzen from Manitoba, Canada enjoys " to interplant everything with a passion for the written word—for poetry."

Heather La Croix: Poet from NM, USA.

Heather Johnson is from MI, USA. "This is definitely not my best work; however, my best works have been turned into song lyrics and rearranged so many times that the originals don't sound or feel right to me anymore. 'Michael The Angel' is about the person who encouraged me to try my hand at writing... I especially want to encourage others to write just for sheer enjoyment!"

H. G. Brown lives in NY, USA; printer, pilot, poet, playwright, grandfather, and happily married man; his excellent poem "On The Bitterroot" appeared in the June Issue of *Taj Mahal Review* (2002).

Hiram Larew: Poet from MD, USA.

Howard Camner: Poet from Florida, USA.

Isadora SuZhen Snapp: Poet from VT, USA.

Jack Conway from MA, USA has been published in *The Antioch Review*; *Light: The Quarterly of Light Verse*. His poems have also appeared in: *Yankee*, *Amelia*; *The New Renaissance*; *The Christian Science Monitor*, *Waveength*; *Poetry Motel*, *Penumbra*, *Eclipse*, *The Hiram Poetry Review* and *The Raven Chronicles*. His work has been anthologized in: *The Norton Anthology of Light Verse*, *The Best Magazine Poetry of 1996*, *The Arvon Foundation International Poetry Anthology*, Ted Hughes and Seamus Heaney, eds. and *The Encyclopedia of New England Culture*. He is the author of several poetry chapbooks. He is a former adjunct professor at Boston University and Fisher College.

J. D. Nelson is a Fine Artist living and writing in the Denver/Boulder, Colorado USA area. He has been performing and recording his lyrics and poetry for more than a decade. He is currently working on new material with ex-members of his former band. His poems appear in the following web journals: Spent Angel Press, Unlikely Stories, remark., Fluid Ink Press, Shadow Poetry, EOTU Ezine, The Shadow Show, The Dream People, Pig Iron Malt and abcdefz.com. In 2002, his work will appear in: *Dirty Pigeon Press, Joey and the Black Boots, Pogonip, Snow Monkey, Thunder Sandwich, Plain Brown Wrapper, Sidereality* and *The Unknown Writer*. He is a loyal fan of the Denver Nuggets.

Jan Oskar Hansen is the renowned poet from Algarve, Portugal. His poems have been published in *The Fabric of A Vision*, *The Still Horizon* and *Taj Mahal Review*.

Jason Clapham: Poet from Kent, UK.

Jason E. Windham: Poet from MS, USA.

Jason McIntosh: Poet from MO, USA.

Jessica Hatton is from NJ, USA. The poet wrote "BLACK TUESDAY" in remembrance of her father, Special Agent Leonard W. Hatton, and all those people who died on September 11. "My father died a hero. He sacrificed his life for the sake of others. May he and all others who died on September 11 rest in peace."

Jessie O'Donovan: Poet from Christchurch, New Zealand.

Jill Chan: Born in Manila, Philippines. Migrated to New Zealand in 1994. Has work published in New Zealand literary journals (*Poetry NZ, Takahe, Spin*, etc.), in on-line zines (*Eclectica, Apples and Oranges, Poetry Magazine, Comrades, Stirring*, etc.) and in the Generation X anthology *In Our Own Words Volume 3*. Edits *PoetrySz: demystifying mental illness*.

Joan Hambidge from South Africa teaches literature at the University of Cape Town; novelist (4 novels); won three literary prizes for poetry.

John A Duffy: Poet from Zomerzet, UK.

John Birkbeck from IA, USA; published in *The Still Horizon*.

John Dempsey: Poet from NY, USA.

John Michael Martinez from Texas, USA is religious, philosophic, trying to figure out why people are so caught up in worldly concepts.

John Western is from Wolverhampton, England; published in various magazines; has written a novel titled *'Slip On Through'* and a book of poetry called *'Orbital Correspondense'*; "Inspired heavily by the 'beat' poets and also Rupert Brooke & Dylan Thomas, Charles Bukowski also."

Joseph Aprile from WA, USA has written many poems, chapbooks, short stories, novellas and novel-length fiction. "I owe my strong attraction to the poetic form to my involvement with the New York Poets Cooperative in the early seventies at that time under the benevolent direction of Barbara Holland. If there is an underlying theme in all of my work, I believe it originates from the desire to understand the human experience and what it means to be human."

Karen Alkalay-Gut: A renowned poet from Israel; published several books of poetry.

Kari Marie Gilbert from IL, USA is a freshman at Pudue University in Indiana, majoring in paleontology.

Kathie Isaac-Luke: Poet from California, USA.

Kathleen K. Harris: Poet from Connecticut, USA.

Kathleen Lawlor: Poet from CT, USA.

Kathleen Rose Cruger: Poet from Illinois, USA.

Prof. (Dr.) Kazuyosi Ikeda (b. 1928) is from Osaka, Japan; D.Sc., D. Litt., bilingual (English/Japanese) poet and scientist; Professor Emeritus of Osaka University; President of International Earth Environment University; a renowned author of numberless poems in "7-5 syllable metre, based on genuine love for all creation; recipient of several awards and listed in 45 famous Who's Who books; published 25 literary works and 50 literary articles; several awards including the International Order of Merit, the Chevalier Grand Cross, International Eminent Poet, Outstanding Man of the 20th Century.

Kenneth McManus: Poet from NY, USA.

Kevin James Knowles: Poet from Illinios, USA.

Kevin M. Horsley from GA, USA offered: "I am a JROTC cadet at Harlem High School. I've achieved the rank of First Lieutenant. I am highly decorated. I am also compassionate and very romantic. I love music, and poetry. I also feel that love is my gift and my curse because I try to treat people with care but when I get hurt I really get hurt."

Kimberly Beth Nelson: Poet from Oregon, USA.

Kirby Wright from CA, USA teaches English Composition at the Art Institute of California and serves as an advisor at National University's Writing Center. He is a past recipient of the Anne Fields Poetry Prize, the Academy of American Poets Award and the Arts Silicon Valley Fellowship in Poetry. His beautiful short story " The Drug Club" appeared in *Taj Mahal Review*.

Kristine: Poet from Stratford, Canada.

Kristina Anna Lehner: Poet from Lauf, Germany.

Kuldeep Kaur: Poet from Jharkhand, India.

Larry Jaffe: Poet from CA, USA.

Lauren Diane Ovsevitz: Poet from Arizona, USA; her excellent poems "Pride" and "Contradiction" appeared in *The Still Horizon* and *Taj Mahal Review*.

Len Rely from VA, USA is an author of speculative fiction including the novel *MONO* now available at Barnes & Noble. He has done poetry, editorial work and local news articles on the side. 75 publications to date.

Les Wicks is from Bondi Junction, Australia. His books *are "The Vanguard Sleeps In"* (Glandular, 1981), *"Cannibals"* (Rochford St, 1985), *"Tickle"* (Island, 1993), *"Nitty Gritty"* (Five Islands, 1997), *"The Ways of Waves"* (Sidewalk, 2000) & *"Appetites of Light"* (Presspress, due 2002). He's performed at festivals, schools, prisons etc. Runs workshops across Australia & is editor of Meuse Press, which focuses on poetry outreach projects.

LeVaughn Flynn is from St. Catherine, Jamaica. "... my poetry is my life. Each poem represents an excerpt of my life and mirrors my experiences that many persons can relate to."

Lee R. Lowder III: Poet from Ohio, USA; published in *The Fabric of A Vision*.

Lee Ennis from Virginia, USA (b. 1952) in Yorktown, Virginia; published both in print and on-line. "At the age of 18, he hit the road with a rock band that he worked with until the age of 30 at which time he met my lovely wife, Dawn. All through the 12 years on the road as a musician, he was doing some freelance writing and photography. Since his marriage to Dawn, he has settled down making writing/photographer a full time endeavor." His poem 'Winter Glow' was published in the June Issue of *Taj Mahal Review* (2002).

Lisa M. Lewis from CA, USA has been writing poetry since the age of 7. "To me, a good poem is one where you can write it even 10 years ago, go back and read it, and it will still evoke the same emotion that caused you to write it."

Lisa-Marie Griffin: Poet from NM, USA.

Lowell Damron: Poet from Ohio, USA.

Louise P. Saltkill is from Arkansas, USA. "I have loved poetry forever! Peaceful, easygoing, and friendly person who relaxes with pen and paper!"

Lucretia Ann Campos: Poet from New Mexico, USA.

Luis Cabalquinto is from New York, USA; lives in Manhattan but divides his writing time between New York City and his birthplace in Magarao, Philippines; writes in three languages (Bikol, Tagalog, English) and his poems have been published in 7 countries. His fourth poetry book *BRIDGEABLE SHORES* was released in the U.S. last year by Kaya Press.

Mandy Dyer: Poet from Essex, UK.

Marek Lugowski is a Polish-born (moved to Chicago, USA when 14 years-old) editor and president of A Small Garlic Press and co-edits with katrina grace craig its online and print poetry serial, *Agnieszka's Dowry* (AgD) ISSN 1088-4300, which can be found at http://www.enteract.com/~asgp/

Maria Cristina Azcona is an Argentine bilingual writer; edited two books of poetry in Argentina and is going to edit her first novel on October 2002; numerous prizes in different contests of poetry in USA and other countries; published in several magazines, anthologies and literary journals.

Maria Theresa Ib is a poet from Vejle, Denmark; a guidance counselor at the University of Southern Denmark Kolding; poems published in both Danish and English since 1999. Among these publications are "*Hvedekorn*" (Danish lit mag, 1999, 2000); "*American Studies in Scnadinavia*" (Academic lit mag, 2001);"*Rain Dog*" (Brit poetry mag 2001); "*Braquemard*" (Brit poetry mag 2001); "*Snakeskin*" (Webzine 2002); "*Writer's Hood*" (Webzine 2002); "*Literary Potpourri*" (Am. webzine 2002); "*Caught in the Net*" (Brit e-zine 2002); "*Transparent Words*" (Brit e-zine 2002).

Marie: Poet from New Hampshire, USA.

Marie Guay: Poet from ID, USA.

Marki Twain: Poet from WA, USA.

Martin A Enticknap from Orkney, UK sends the following bio: "Father of Cassie, author *of Exodus: The Dolph/in Saga*, and computer graphic artist, (Novel Covers) and a writer of poetry since the age of 14. Apart from being a Dad my other consistent love is poetry, and enjoy writing them even if no one else will ever read them. But it is great to share a moment of movement in our souls journey."

Mary Kathryn Cannon is from Delaware, USA; Writer/poet/Author Certified member of the Youth and Families Child Inc; nominated Two Thousand Notable Women 1992, Five Thousand Personalities of the World; Silver and Golden Poet award by World of poetry; writings contributed to *Boys Town*, *The Convenant House The Montel Williams Show* and *Save Our Children Coalition Org*; published works in various anthologies.

Matthew Johnson from CA, USA says: "In a confusing world of countless thoughts and emotions we are overwhelmed with organizing the almost impossible. That's the reason people are musician's, poet's, artists, etc. Ways to express emotions and organize them. In my writings I hope to connect to similar beings with the same views as I. To use the essence of simplicity in our life, it is important to become natural with that way of life."

Melisande Luna from California, USA wrote: "I enjoy the subtle art of poetry, building the emotional tension of the words, crafting tactile sensations that reach out and physically grasp the reader is what excites me most about the process of creative writing."

MercyRain from PA, USA is a janitor while trying to eke out a career as a poet and painter; work has appeared in various magazines and zines including *Comrades, Atomic Petals, Megaera* and others. "A devout believer in chaos, Mercy's life goal is to disprove anything that has been proven."

Michael D. Petti from NY, USA "is a married father of two children. A hopeless romantic whose upbringing in Brooklyn, NY helps to ground him in reality."

Michael J Shepard is from Texas, USA. "Life has taught me much thus far, and my experiences help me to express myself with my "pen," be it an actual pen or my computer."

Michael Levy is from Florida, USA; articles and poems on over 1500 web sites, journals and magazines; latest story published in "*Chicken Soup for the Jewish Soul*"; appeared on hundreds of radio programs, Channel 4TV in the U K and recently a live interview on NBC 6 in the USA; a guest on the Howard Stern; a guest lecturer on the maiden transatlantic voyage of the Norwegian Sun; *Invest With A Genius* published in January 2002; *Truths of The Soul* is due shortly.

Michael R. Collings: Poet from CA, USA.

Michael Paul Chmielecki: Poet from CA, USA.

Michelle Dunk-Martin: Poet from MI, USA.

Mike Subritzky from Waikato, New Zealand "is regarded internationally as the 'Kiwi Kipling' and writes his war poetry in the gritty, in your face style of the barrack room and the forward trench."

Mukunda Tom Stiles: Poet from CO, USA.

Natasha C. Burroughs: Poet from AL, USA. "I'm a RN specializing in HIV care. I discovered poetry as a way of therapy to help with my everyday emotions. It is so important that the soul of me is pure and honest and reflects God the Father in me. My writings are a product of that daily struggle."

Nguyen Duc Batngan from Alberta, Canada wrote: "This poem translated by Andy Kale Original title: Xuong Trang From: "Binh Minh Cam" (Shrouded Dawn) A collection of poetry written in 1975 published in 1985."

Nicholas Gallimore: Poet from NY, USA.

Dr. Nilanshu Kumar Agrawal is from UP, India. He is Ph.D. in English and Senior Lecturer in English at a P.G. College in UP, affiliated with CSJM University, India. The topic of his doctoral dissertation is *"T.S.Eliot's Poetry In The Light of His Critical Thoughts"*. His "Tempest of Passion" is a prize-winning poem.

Olaf Korder was born in 1949 in the Netherlands; writing poems and stories since 1968; published in *The Still Horizon* and *Taj Mahal Review*; you can read his work (in Dutch and English) on his own site http://www.literatuur.nu/~korder.

Olukoga Tayo: Poet from Oyo, Nigeria.

Dr. Padmore Agbemabiese is from Ghana in West Africa; lives in OH, USA; one of Ghana's young poets, playwright, and journalist; started writing in his native Ewe language at the age of 10 to entertain Church members on weekends; collection of Ewe poems published in two volumes for use by the Non-Formal Education Program in Ghana. Between 1980 and 1997, Padmore had Poetry Night on the national Radio Station every Saturday evening from 8:00 PM to 9:00 PM; currently, in The Ohio State University, College of Education; poems translated in four languages; published in 11 anthologies, including *Essence Magazine* (December, 2001); *Culture Elixir* (2000); *Rhapsody* (1999); *The Fabric of A Vision* in India (2001); *The Still Horizon* in India (2002) etc.

Page Malbrough from New Jersey, USA has been the three year Writer-in-Residence at Open Space Arts, a non-profit organization, writing scripts and poems while teaching her creative writing group the Young Writers' Guild. Her poetry has been published most recently in Morturi. She currently lives in New Jersey, USA with her husband Michael.

Pat Phillips West is a former hospital administrator/business owner/office manager who lives, and writes in northern Nevada, USA. Her work has appeared in the anthology *Labyrinth: Poems and Prose*, and Ezines such as FZQ Poetry, Poetictricity, and Kota Press.

Patricia Gomes is a famous poet from Massachusetts, USA. "Poetry clears the cobwebs from my mind. It affords the opportunity to cleanse the thoughts and sort through the muck..."

Patricia H. Regensburg: Poet from Maine, USA.

Patricia Wellingham-Jones, a renowned poet, lives in Northern California; a former psychology researcher/writer/editor who has been widely published in journals, newspapers, anthologies, and online magazines. Her most recent books are *Don't Turn Away: Poems About Breast Cancer*, *Labyrinth: Poems & Prose*, and the forthcoming Lummox Press Little Red Book, *A Gathering Glance*.

R.A.Munoz is a twenty seven-year old Latin American poet living in Fort Wayne, Indiana. "I have written poetry for as long as I have been able to hold a pen or pencil.... My poetry is never meant to be rude or crass, those areas are far too cheap and easily found on many a bathroom wall. I would rather hope that my works provoke thought, conversation and if able, inspiration to those who feel they have not yet found a voice of their own."

Richard James Allen from NSW, Australia is a poet, performer, choreographer, and filmmaker. His poetry, performance texts, and cross media works have been published, broadcast, performed and screened widely. His seventh book of poetry, *"Thursday's Fictions"* (Five Island Press), was shortlisted for the 2000 NSW Premier's Literary Award for Poetry. His recent monologue, *"More Lies"*, presented by the 2000 Sydney Writers Festival, was shortlisted for the 2001 Griffin Award for New Australian Playwriting. In 1999 he co-edited with Karen Pearlman the landmark collection, *"Performing the Unnameable: An Anthology of Australian Performance Texts"* (Currency Press/ RealTime). Richard has been a judge of numerous performance poetry competitions. He has recently completed a number of short films for his company, The Physical TV Company. These include: *"Rubberman Accepts The Nobel Prize"*, which he co-wrote and starred in, shortlisted for the Best Dance Film at the 2001 Australian Dance Awards; and *"No Surrender"*, which he wrote and directed (based on the poem submitted), broadcast on ABC TV and winner of an 2002 ATOM Award for Best Experimental Film. Visit his website www.artmedia.com.au/physical tv.htm.

Richard Paul Crowther: Poet from Sheffield, England.

Richard Stevenson has read to enthusiastic audiences across the country; the author of thirteen full-length collections of poetry, including, most recently, *A Murder of Crows: New & Selected Poems*, *Live Evil: Homage To Miles Davis*, *Nothing Definite Yeti* (YA verse), and *Hot Flashes: Maiduguri Haiku, Senryu, and Tanka;* also performs with the young adult rock/ poetry group

Sasquatch and the adult jazz/poetry ensemble Naked Ear, which recently recorded a CD, *See 4/4 Mile;* regularly reviews poetry and fiction, and periodically runs adult and young adult workshops; holds degrees in English and Creative Writing from The University of Victoria and University of British Columbia and teaches Canadian Literature, Creative Writing, and Business Communication at Lethbridge Community College in southern Alberta.

Rickey K. Hood was born in Charlotte, NC, USA on Dec. 29, 1960; proud to be a native Charlottean, poet, and essayist; a nationally and internationally published poet as well as an award-winning journalist for the Black Reign Newspaper published in New York City; included in the Marquis: Who's Who in America, 2001 edition and Who's Who in America Special 2002 edition; first volume of poetry entitled, In a Little Corner of a Black Man's Mind Stand I..., won Recognition from the North Carolina Association of Educator's Minority Arts Contest, 1997; received his A. A. Degree from Central Piedmont Community College and is now working on his B. A. Degree in Religion and Philosophy at the University of North Carolina at Charlotte.

Rina Ferrarelli from Pennsylvania, USA supplied the following bio: "I am a poet and translator who taught English and translation theory at the college level for many years. I have published widely in journals and anthologies and have a chapbook and a full-length book of original poetry and two books of translation."

Robert Edgar Burns from FL, USA is "a 49 year old retired law enforcement officer, who not only writes poetry and short stories, but is a gifted artist as well having won many awards on a National basis and had been writing poetry since the age of 8 years old. Robby is related to the Scottish poet of the same name."

Robert L. Jackson from GA, USA has published his poetry in several literary publications across America. He now also has a book published entitled "Shedding Layers of Ocean." He is also a graduate student in the school of Mechanical Engineering at Georgia Tech, in Atlanta, GA, USA. See www.saltlines.com for info.

Rodney Kuhn: Poet from Indiana, USA.

Roland Leach, an Australian poet with three books of poetry published, is a winner of major poetry prizes in Australia - Newcastle Prize 1995 and Josephine Ulrich Prize in 1998.

Rolland G. Smith is a journalist and poet from New York, USA; author of two poetry books *Quiet Musings* and *Encore - The Poetry of Nature.*

Romus Simpson from CA, USA sends the following bio: "Poet living and working in Central California. The veteran of more than 350 performances and a very good friend. I have been in love three times, twice to the same woman. I think poetry is the language of God and books are His residence."

Ron Cole from CT, USA lives in Southern Connecticut; has a BS in English/ Secondary Ed; currently working towards an MS, attends poetry readings; surfs the poetry websites and tries to read as much new poetry as he can; favorite poets are the Romantics; working on first book of poems.

Rosa M. DelVecchio from Ohio, USA is Ph.D. in English, Case Western Reserve University, 1993.

Ross Conrad Galvan: Poet from Texas, USA.

Rune Leknes: Poet from Fyllingsdalen, Norway; published in *The Fabric of A Vision* and *The Still Horizon*.

Ruth Daigon is from CA, USA; founder and editor of *Poets On*; won The Eve of St. Agnes Award (Negative Capability) 1993; poetry collections titled *"Between One Future And The Next"* (Papier-Mache Press) 1995. *"About A Year"* (Small Poetry Press in 1996), *"The Moon Inside"*; *"Handfuls of Time"* is due shortly. Dagon's poetry awards include "The Ann Stanford Poetry Prize", 1997 (University of Southern California Anthology, 1998) and The Greensboro Poetry Award (Greensboro Arts Council, 2000). In her previous life as a concert singer she was soprano soloist with the New York Pro Musica (renaissance music), collaborated with W.H. Auden on a recording of Elizabethan Verse and Music for Columbia Records. Ruth Daigon has recently won several chapbook contests as part of anthology series (Kota Press, Three Candles)

Saaleha Bamjee: Poet from Gauteng, South Africa.

Salvatore Amico M. Buttaci from New Jersey, USA is an English teacher at a local middle school and an adjunct professor at a nearby community college. "My poems and stories have appeared in numerous publications in America and in other countries. I live with the love of my life, Sharon, my wife."

Dr. Santosh Kumar: (b. 1946) is from UP India; Head of the English Department in A.D. College, Allahabad; Ph.D. in English; several awards; poems published in many anthologies; awarded for writing an epic *The Fire and The Garden: An Exploration of Beauty* in three volumes.

Sean David Gregson from CA, USA sends the bio: "Citizen of the earth. Seeker of the afterlife. Cherisher of beauty. Gate Chief for the Angels."

Sean Nugent from FL, USA is a "part time poet, novelist." "If you write from your heart then your poems will always be masterpieces of art, they may not be a Picaso painting but never the less they'll be masterpieces heavenly works of art in their own regard."

Serge van Duijnhoven (born 1970 in Oss, in the south of the Netherlands) is a performing poet, novelist, playwright and art-editor from Vlaams Brabant, Belgium. He is the author of several books of fiction and non-fiction. Among them four books of poems: The Palace of Sleep (1993), Copycat (1996), End of the Line: Phantom City (1997), Obiit in Orbit; at the other end of the night (1999). In the last books, cd's are included with musical recordings from his band 'Poets Don't Dance'. In the fall of 1999 his latest book of non-fiction was published: We call them Roses, a collection of personal impressions gathered during five years of travelling through the tormented Balkan regions of former Yugoslavia. The book reached the longlist of the 'Gouden Uil Literatuurprijs 2000' (Golden Owl Literature Price of Flanders). During the war in Bosnia, Serge lived for a while in Sarajevo.

Shabnam Abdoola: Poet from Gauteng, South Africa.

Shalini Nayar: Poet from Wilayah Persekutuan, Malaysia.

Sharon W. Flynn from MA, USA, wrote: "My Poetry has appeared in a number of journals such a Lucidity, Poets Magazine, Parnassus Literary Journal. My biography was included in the Eighth and Ninth International Cyclopedia of Who's Who In Poetry. I am the mother of four, grandmother of four. I am currently working on a collection of Native American and Nature poems. "Spirit Flute Unending" uses the Native American spirit-flute image to show the eternal in a true and lasting love."

Shawnte Orion resides in Surprise, AZ and was a finalist for Arizona State Poetry Society and Writer's Foundation awards. His poetry was recently published in The Peralta Press, Red Booth Review, Facets Magazine and Premiere Generation Ink and is forthcoming in Stickman Review and Branches Quarterly.

Sherri Anderson: Poet from TN, USA.

Sheryl Mackiernan: Poet from Massachusetts, USA.

Shirley Bolstok lives in Denver, Colorado in the United States; has appeared in numerous publications including *The Fabric of A Vision, The Still Horizon* and *Taj Mahal Review*.

Shivendra N Green: Poet from GA, USA.

Sonia Edwards from California, USA wrote: "I am a young poet but I love what I do. All my poems tell a story. Tell how I feel, or what has happened in my life. Poetry is not just something, it is one of God's gifts to us."

Stanislaus Jaworski: Poet from The Hague, The Netherlands.

Steve Murray from Yorkshire, a poet from the north of England, has been published on a number of occasions. He is keen on getting unread poets to the forefront, and would love to see someone with money promote poetry and young poets, bringing this, I believe dying art, back to life. He feels "there are a fantastic number of talented poets out there who should be entertaining the masses, rather than twelve people in a library who have only gone there because there is free coffee and biscuits."

Steven Valentine: Poet from Swindon, England; collection of poems can be viewed at www.allaboutsteve.co.uk.

Stuart Jason Deutsch from North Dakota, USA says: "I am married with one child who just turned 1 yr. old. I seek to write inspiring poetry that gives people a positive outlook on life and helps them feel good in a dark world. I want to write things which give people hope and help them persevere through the challenges life presents."

Sudheesh V Nair from CA, USA is a computer networking professional working in Silicon Valley. His excellent poem "Moon Singing Life" appeared in *The Fabric of A Vision* (2001).

Susan K. Rowse from Georgia, USA provided: "I am a southern woman of grace with the rebellious nature instilled in me from a family rich in heritage and pride. I live along the southeast coast of Dixie and enjoy nature with all her treasures. I love the water and sky and feel comforted by the blanket afforded me in every detail of living."

Susie Davies lives with her partner Dean and his three Children in Essex, England. She has been writing poetry since she was a small child and has also recently been working on her first novel.

Taylor Graham from CA, USA is a volunteer search-and-rescue dog handler in the California Sierra, and also helps her husband (a retired wildlife biologist) with his bird projects. Her poetry has appeared in America, International Poetry Review, The Iowa Review, Poetry International and elsewhere.

Thelma Shutters from Missouri, USA wrote: "I am a mother of 5 and grandmother of 12. I started writing March 1st this year after I had given my three sisters a porcelain angel that I had prayed on. After I had given it to them I just all of a sudden wrote PORCELAIN ANGEL then the poems just kept coming. I know it was a Miracle from GOD."

Thomas Fortenberry from North Carolina, USA is an American author, editor, and publisher. Owner of Mind Fire Press, he has judged many literary contests, including The Georgia Author of the Year Awards and The Robert Penn Warren Prize for Fiction. His work has appeared internationally in publications such as Amelia, Cicada, Maelstrom, Contemporary Southern Poets of 1997, Poetry Magazine, Writer's Choice, Fiction Network, Soul Unmade, Poetry Superhighway, Ariga, Eternity, Gravity, Uno, Lower Than the Angels, Wooden Head Review, Poetry Depth Qaurterly, Lumi Virtuale, The European Legacy, and is forthcoming as the introduction on a new edition of H. G. Wells' The Outline of History.

Timothy McNeal (b.1944) is from Alzey, Germany. The poet's publications are "Albedo" (Poems in German & English / Germany 1993), "Twilight" (Poems / USA / 1996), Featured Poet 1995 (USA), Featured International Writer 1997 (USA), The Zone Poetry Contest Winner 2001 (USA), The Arts Angels Poetry Competition Winner 2002 (CDN).

Tina K Campbell was born in Essex, England, and lives in Kent with her parents and brother. She is currently studying at Welling School. Her dream is to study at Warwick University. The poet adds, "After that, the sweet morning sky is bountiful and the night's shining star her compass."

Todd Burge: Poet from WV, USA.

Tony Bush is from Powys, UK "Married with 2 children, failed romantic (some would say cynic) and a poetry enthusiast… a book of poetry and modern art (art by UK painter/sculptor Nelson Nanson) launched in June 2002." Visit the poet at http://tonybush.esmartweb.com.

Tony Weaver: Poet from Missouri, USA.

Torey Fraley: Poet from MD, USA.

Troels Hundtofte: Poet from Aarhus, Denmark; loves music and poetry.

Uppalapati Lakshmi Prasanthi: Poet from Andhra Pradesh, India.

Venessa Aquilla Hall is from GA, USA; loves writing poems, riding horses. The poet also teaches herself "with a lot of praying how to play electric piano." Her beautiful poem "Demented" appeared in *The Still Horizon*.

W. S. Mayo: Poet from MD, USA.

Ward Kelley: Poet from IN, USA.

William Dean Hamilton: Poet from Iowa, USA. He is a published author with eleven of his poems published, and seven of his short stories, and one book and a non-fiction essay.

William James Jenkinson was born in Scotland; lives in Evanston, Australia; "Picture From Yesterday" published in *The Fabric of A Vision*; three poems appeared in an International Journal *Taj Mahal Review*; writing poetry provides "an outlet for my passions."

Yvonne Sparkes from Essex, England writes, "I am a semi retired nurse to the elderly. I lived in New York until 1958... I am very happy when people read and like my poetry. It brings us closer together with like experiences. My poetry reflects my feelings, and experience of life." Her three poems were anthologized in *The Still Horizon*.